WHAT PEOPLE ARE SAYING ABOUT *BE UNSHAKEN* . . .

"Having followed Dr. Tiffany's work for years, I can attest that her thoughtful perspective makes this book stand out. Her ability to break down this powerful topic and the strategies of exceptional leaders is nothing short of inspiring."

—Debbie Blas, Director of the Engaged Learning and Career Action Center for Students, Washington State University Vancouver

"Dr. Brandreth's work is foundational for any leader who is seeking to create and sustain meaningful change. She lays out a functional framework for leadership that is authentic, purpose-driven, and transformational. A true handbook for creating leadership impact."

—Jared Smith, SHRM-SCP, MS-HRD, Director of HR Operations, Compass Minerals

"*Be Unshaken* is a master class in resilient leadership. Dr. Tiffany Brandreth reveals how the world's most effective leaders rise above uncertainty and turn pivotal moments into powerful transformations. This book is a must-read for anyone who wants to lead with clarity, strength, and unwavering purpose."

—Jim Madrid, mindset expert, performance coach to professional athletes & world-class teams, author, keynote speaker, and stage 4 cancer survivor, Madrid Partners LLC

"*Be Unshaken* is a powerful and honest exploration of the realities of leadership. Dr. Brandreth challenges leaders to confront the uncomfortable truths that often go unspoken. My takeaway, as Dr. Brandreth has long taught me, is that truth-telling is a true catalyst for change. Genuine organizational transformation begins when leaders are willing to speak and hear the truth—even when it is uncomfortable. Great read for leaders at all levels."

—Angie Draves, SHRM-CP, Director of Human Resources, Elliot Aviation

"Master class is often an overused term, but not here! This is truly a master class in what separates leaders who react from those who rise."

—Michael Alder, trial lawyer and community leader, Alder Law, ZA Lawyers, East LA YMCA, voted Top 100 Lawyer in California

"In pivotal moments, leaders need a method—not a mantra. Dr. Brandreth's 5×5 model has become my go-to protocol in conflict—steadying the room, focusing on facts and commitments, and moving teams from reaction to reflection to resolution."

—Lisa Pitters, MBA, Chief Education Officer, Five Keys

"I had the privilege of working with Dr. T when she led unforgettable sessions on inclusion and belonging in my organization. Reading *Be Unshaken* reaffirms what I've always known—she lives the principles she teaches, bringing authenticity and courage to every conversation. Her insights are a timely call to action for leaders who want to create meaningful change."

—Jeanine Dooley, Supply Chain Transformation Director, Corporate Engagement Champion for Inclusion, Diversity, and Belonging, Diageo

"I've had the privilege of working with Dr. Tiffany and have seen firsthand how even the most capable executives struggle to sustain difficult conversations when ego feels threatened. The four archetypes of purpose-driven leaders she introduces are grounded in research and spot on! Her work reveals why only 10% of leaders truly achieve transformative results. *Be Unshaken* is, without question, one of the most important leadership books of our time."

—Carmen Kaufenberg, Senior Finance Professional, MPA, Sunburst Memorials

"I love the flow of this book! It's succinct and follows a clear pathway for leadership that highlights the true avenues to deepen self-awareness while revealing the great responsibility that comes with leading others. I would follow this book to the "T" . . . as Dr. "T"iffany has been an absolute inspiration to me both professionally and personally, in my own pathway in business and how I view leadership."

—JJ Fogle, Managing Partner, Totus Wealth Management

BE UNSHAKEN

How the **Top 10%** of Leaders
Transform Themselves and Their
Companies in Pivotal Moments

DR. TIFFANY BRANDRETH

Be Unshaken: How the Top 10% of Leaders Transform Themselves and Their Companies in Pivotal Moments
Dr. Tiffany Brandreth © 2025

Hardcover ISBN: 978-1-61206-383-6
Softcover ISBN: 978-1-61206-384-3
eBook ISBN: 978-1-61206-385-0
Audiobook ISBN: 978-1-61206-386-7

For more information, visit DrTiffanyBrandreth.com

To purchase this book at quantity discounts, contact Aloha Publishing at alohapublishing@gmail.com

Published by:

aloha
PUBLISHING

AlohaPublishing.com

Printed in the United States of America

DEDICATION

This book is dedicated to the leaders who invited me into their lives—those who shared their experiences in one-on-one conversations, entrusted me with their stories during focus groups and surveys, and welcomed me into their executive teams during seasons of challenge and change. Whether spoken in private or expressed in the safety of collective spaces, your truth shaped the very foundation of this work.

To every leader, team, and organization I've supported, thank you for allowing me into the spaces where real leadership is tested and revealed. Your willingness to lean in to discomfort, to wrestle with hard truths, and to pursue something more meaningful has shaped not only this body of work, but the very way I understand leadership itself. You've taught me through your courage, your commitments, and even your contradictions, and I mean that in a positive way. And thank you for the trust you placed in me along the way, for the lessons you never knew you were teaching, and for the wisdom I carry forward because of you. I am deeply grateful.

My hope is this book honors that trust, affirms the impact you seek to make, and offers something in return: hope, new answers, and a path forward into a future that will challenge what feels familiar and safe. And when you arrive at the inevitable crossroads—where the choice between self-preservation or purpose stands before you—I hope this gives you the clarity and courage to choose your purpose. Because that choice becomes a turning point for your life, your legacy, and the imprint you leave in helping make the world better.

CONTENTS

INTRODUCTION

"Will this be kept confidential?"

It's the question I hear more than any other, not only from employees or middle managers, but from executives, equity partners, and members of the C-suite. It's a moment that always comes before the truth is shared. A checkpoint before someone takes the risk of speaking honestly about what they've seen, what they've felt, and what they've lived at work.

This question doesn't just signal fear. It exposes a deeper reality: even in rooms full of power, people feel powerless to speak honestly. They want to know the conversation is protected. That what they say won't be traced back to them because it could threaten their job, their income, their reputation, or their future.

Over time, I came to understand I was being entrusted with the untold stories of the workplace: the truths leaders couldn't admit in public, the contradictions between what a company claimed to value and what it actually practiced, or the gap between the mission on the wall and the behavior in the halls.

So why is truth so dangerous? It's not that it's destructive; it's that it disrupts. Even when truth serves the business or advances the mission, it's treated like a threat. And that fear—whether it's perceived or reinforced by real consequences—is the origination point by which all change efforts unravel. In nearly every organization I've worked with, this is where the progress collapses: not for lack of vision, but because the truth can't be spoken. And when the truth can't be spoken, nothing can shift, progress, or evolve.

Throughout this book, you'll hear stories from inside the boardroom and behind closed doors. You'll see how leaders with the best of intentions lose their influence. You'll recognize the patterns that slowly erode and stall change—not because they're hard to detect, but because they're rarely discussed.

This isn't about pointing fingers. It's about reclaiming the power of truth in leadership. Because when leaders learn how to receive it, act on it, and lead with it—even in the face of risk—they become the ones who not only navigate change, but drive transformation.

Nearly 15 years ago, I started my consulting firm, not because I had a grand plan, but because advocating for the fair and healthy treatment of employees inside the very consulting firm I was entrusted to help lead ultimately cost me my vice president role—a role where I had planned to commit for the entirety of my career. I had spent years working tirelessly to help CEOs—leaders who inspired me with their vision and values—grow their businesses. Behind closed doors, I saw a different reality—leaders acting against their stated values and fostering toxic environments for the very people they sought to empower. Even more troubling, the same leadership concepts we were teaching others—communication, inclusion, and values-driven culture—were being violated within our own firm.

At the time, I didn't fully understand the dynamics of truth and power. "Speaking truth to power" wasn't a widespread concept the way it is today. I just knew the culture was off, the conditions were unlawful, and that we could be better.

I was knee-deep in preparing to present the employee survey results on the day I was let go, not because I wasn't doing my job, but because I was giving others a way to share their thoughts and challenges. The entire company quit that same day—but that's an incredible story for another time. What mattered was the glaring contradiction between what we preached and what was practiced. It wasn't about long hours. It wasn't about typical workplace challenges. It was about an egregious abuse of power—especially toward the younger staff members. That disconnect didn't just feel wrong. It was wrong.

It's true what they say—when a door closes, a window opens.

Starting my own firm wasn't something I felt naturally comfortable doing. I valued the stability of a consistent paycheck and the connection that came from being part of a team. So when the moment came, it was a true turning point. I took a chance—not with certainty, but with conviction that there had to be a better way to lead. One guided by a single, uncompromising rule: walk the talk. It wasn't about being perfect. It was about being congruent.

What I couldn't have predicted was this early commitment to credibility and congruence would form the foundation of my work with leadership teams, fuel my research, and ignite the question that has stayed with me for over a decade:

Why do leaders, despite their best intentions, abandon their commitment to creating change?

This question has been asked and answered in countless ways. Yet applying those answers kept producing the same result: failed progress, broken trust, and stalled change. I knew I had to look deeper. Not for better frameworks or better language, but to un-cover the *real* reason change efforts were collapsing at the moment they were most needed.

Over the next decade, I worked alongside leaders at every level: those striving to grow personally, those trying to shift dynamics within their teams, and those driving entire organizations through large-scale change. Whether personal or organizational, the goal was the same: to bridge the gap between where they were and the impact they aspired to make.

Again and again, I saw a familiar pattern: the most purpose-driven leaders, those genuinely committed to doing better, would quit prematurely. Their actions, decisions, and interactions would eventually betray the very values they wanted to champion.

And almost every time, the same two phrases would surface in my confidential meetings:

"Will this be kept confidential?"

"They will never change."

These two phrases became recurring themes in my work. They pointed to something deeper, something systemic: a leadership culture built on self-protection, where change could halt without consequence, shielded by NDAs.

I work in those rooms, at these tables where the real decisions get made. Not the ones published in memos or shared at all-hands meetings. The ones no one hears about, but everyone feels.

I remember one executive team in particular. An organization brought me in after a series of public resignations and escalating internal conflict. A new CEO had taken the helm and the executive team insisted it was time for a cultural reset. I was told they were ready to "do the real work."

But early on, the signs were familiar: hesitation, guarded language, discomfort when tough topics surfaced. In our first session, I asked them what had gone unspoken the longest. Silence followed. Eventually, someone offered a safe response about "miscommunication," and the rest of the group nodded. They weren't ready.

So we moved at the pace they needed. Session after session, trust was built, doing real work through safe hypotheticals. Eventually, we arrived at a discussion I always know will surface: *What leads people to say, "They'll never change?"*

The CEO asked me, *"Are they saying that about us? Please tell us the truth."*

Every head nodded in agreement. They wanted to know. When this moment arrives, it signifies a turning point. They had worked through their own power struggles and reached a place where they could engage the truth without it causing conflict or consequences to their careers.

Anther executive asked the same question, *"Are they saying that about us? That we'll never change?"*

I answered delicately but in a straightforward way. *Yes*, it was being said—and I explained *why*. Not as criticism, but as context. It's a sentiment that doesn't form overnight or from isolated incidents. It's built over time, through real stories and real scenarios that go unaddressed.

That opened the door. Their own stories began to surface: of people overlooked for promotions without explanation, of leaders who labeled feedback as insubordination, of priorities that shifted depending on who was in the room. They weren't just hearing it. They were seeing it. We had made incremental breakthroughs before, but this was different. This was a leap forward!

That night, I received calls from those who felt they had the least power in the group feeling grateful, relieved, and optimistic.

But the next session, two executives were absent. Their assistants cited "scheduling conflicts." Within a week, I received a call: the engagement was "on pause." No follow-up. A post-session debrief was a regular practice after each session. This time it was avoided. That pause became permanent.

Not because the team didn't care but because they reached the threshold where change got personal. And in the absence of consequence, the most powerful people in the room can simply choose to opt out. That's where change begins to unravel.

This is the pattern.

There is always high engagement with the work and high trust with me. Work phones stay silenced. Laptops stay closed. Whispers of *"We've never had our attention held for this long."*

Until leaders realize the change isn't just for their teams. It's for *them* as well. And once that truth hits, resistance sets in. Not loudly. It comes quietly, as a calendar block that never gets rescheduled.

But the impact is anything but quiet.

It leaves those who believed—those who took the risk to speak up and hoped for something better—disillusioned once again. I witnessed organizations rally behind the promise of real change, only to retreat the moment real change demanded more than rhetoric. Leaders who had sworn commitment to bold initiatives abandoned them as soon as the stakes became personal.

And this isn't about one team, or one industry. It's a recurring failure I've witnessed across sectors in local, regional, national, and global reach.

When fear is activated, ego speaks louder than purpose.

Through years of grounded theory research and rigorous analysis, I studied these moments—not as outliers, but as patterns. Quiet turning points where even purpose-driven leaders, with the best intentions, abandoned what they said they were committed to, for the tens, hundreds, or thousands they lead.

And the result is always the same: they may quit at different phases, but the expiration date of the commitment arrives. Change ends prematurely and the status quo is preserved. What's lost are the very things that inspired change in the first place. Competitive edge. Market expansion. Cultural alignment. Strategic execution.

And on a personal level? Aspirations are shelved. Convictions are diluted. For some, feelings of hopelessness, helplessness, or powerlessness takes hold. For others, cynicism and contempt set in. The kind of leader they *intended* to be is gradually replaced by the one who chose to play it safe, rationalized by reasons that avoid responsibility.

Not because they were bad people. Not because they lacked care or competence. Because they didn't see or anticipate that moment coming. And when it arrived, ego made the choice for them.

At one point, I came close to walking away from this work entirely.

It started taking a toll and weighed heavily on my heart. I imagined the disappointment others were feeling. Those who had bravely shared their stories, who trusted their voices would matter, only to be met with silence and inaction. As their voices were ignored and their hopes were completely let down, I carried that weight with me. It forced me to ask a question—not about whether I *could* keep doing this work, but whether I *should*.

If I couldn't protect people from being let down, was I complicit in giving them hope?

It became a matter of my own integrity.

After a decade of seeing leaders retreat—either from speaking up or after being spoken to—I set out to find an answer to these questions:

If purpose is meant to drive change, why isn't it enough? Why, despite their purpose, do even the best leaders still abandon the work?

On my journey, I made a discovery that changed everything:

Leaders will abandon their higher purpose the moment their instinct to self-protect outweighs their commitment to a mission greater than themselves.

As a result, 90% of change initiatives fail because well-intentioned, purpose-driven individuals abandon their commitment to change and their higher purpose when personal security is at stake.

THE LIMITS OF PURPOSE

We've been sold the idea that knowing your purpose and leading with it is the key to impactful leadership. I believed this too. I helped thousands of leaders identify and define their purpose, guiding them to lead in alignment with it. But reality tells a more complex story.

Leaders assume their sense of purpose will anchor them, but I discovered that when their stability is threatened—when status, financial security, or key relationships are at risk—their ego takes over. It doesn't happen in an obvious, deliberate way, but in a way that feels almost second nature—an unconscious shift, an instinctive pull toward self-preservation. Suddenly, compromises seem

justifiable, difficult conversations are avoided, and decisions prioritize personal security over the greater mission.

Purpose, it turns out, is not an automatic safeguard against fear.
Why? When identity, authority, or stability feel threatened, the
amygdala—the brain's survival center—hijacks decision-making.
It's this instinctual fear response that dictates choices before leaders
even recognize what's happening.

This is how purpose is abandoned—through a four-step pattern
leaders often fall into when the truth feels threatening.

1. A GAP IS EXPOSED

Unfavorable information comes to light—whether through feedback, data, or direct observation—revealing a disconnect between a
leader's intent and the actual impact.

2. THE THREAT IS FELT

The discomfort of exposure triggers internal defensiveness. Rather
than leaning into these insights, the leader experiences it as a threat
to identity, security, and comfort.

3. EGO TAKES CONTROL

Self-protection becomes the default response. As a result, the ego
jumps into the driver's seat, and pushes purpose into the back seat.
Now, ego has taken the wheel.

4. POWER IS MISUSED

And this is when leaders will misuse their power, not out of malice,
but out of protection. They either dismiss, deflect, or invalidate information that exposes any possible vulnerabilities in their leadership.

This is what surprised me the most about my research.

Purpose does not protect leaders from their ego. Leaders will abandon their purpose when their power, position, or favor feels in jeopardy.

WHEN EGO THREATENS PURPOSE

There are three most common threats that create a complex dilemma for leaders. This is where the true pressure surfaces, where the higher purpose, strategic mission, and long-term aspirations become the most vulnerable. And it's in these moments the instinct to self-protect is at its strongest, overriding what the business truly needs.

1. HEARING TRUTH WHILE HOLDING POWER

One of the greatest responsibilities of—and threats to—a leader's purpose is how they respond when uncomfortable truths are spoken to them. Hearing these truths often disrupts a leader's comfort zone. The feedback may call out specific behaviors, team dynamics, or systemic issues within the organization. For the leader, it can feel like a threat, particularly when they're accustomed to being liked, popular, or the wisest person in the room.

Leaders hold immense power over others' careers, opportunities, and professional stability. How they react to truth—especially when it challenges their self-perception—determines whether they build trust or erode it.

I recall a situation involving two C-suite executives of a prominent organization who were faced with evidence of troubling behavior from one of their closest colleagues. This colleague was celebrated for her exceptional ability to raise funds and her deep connections within their industry. Her contributions were undeniable, and she was considered a cornerstone of the organization's achievements. She and the CEO shared a long-standing friendship, bonded by their experience as pioneers in a male-dominated industry and their shared commitment to uplifting women.

However, cracks in this image emerged when female employees began raising concerns about a pattern of inappropriate remarks toward them. She made comments that were demeaning to younger female staff, questioned the work ethic of those balancing motherhood and careers, and reinforced harmful stereotypes about women's capabilities and commitment in the workplace.

Despite these incidents being brought to the executive team's attention, their response was to defend her. They insisted these remarks weren't reflective of her "true character," dismissing the information as misunderstandings rather than addressing the impact of her behavior. They were more focused on protecting her reputation—and, by extension, their own—than acknowledging the harm being caused.

This loyalty to one another and to the image they had come to embody, took precedence over the values they pledged to uphold. The unspoken allegiance distorted the team's internal dynamics and the control didn't stop there. Male-bashing, done in jest, had become so normalized in public settings that it was backfiring. What began as light commentary was turning advocates into silent dissenters.

Some men felt conflicted, recognizing their inherent privilege, yet insulted in the very spaces where they were trying to support change.

The CEO maintained near-total control behind closed doors, and her colleague actively sustained that dynamic, while presenting a public narrative of collaboration, empowerment, and shared leadership.

The result was a growing disconnect between the organization's public commitment and its internal reality. Employees and members viewed the leadership's efforts as performative, reinforcing the belief that their commitment to culture change wasn't genuine but for show.

Whispers of, *"They will never change,"* spread throughout the organization. The unwillingness to acknowledge these grievances sent a clear and troubling message: change was welcome only when it didn't threaten the dynamics that preserved power and control.

The leadership's message lost its impact, seen as empty rhetoric rather than a true commitment to change. Fear of professional repercussions kept those who participated silent. Even those who believed in the stated ideals weren't willing to risk their referrals, relationships, or reputations to rock the boat. In a system where access and opportunity functioned as currency, preserving one's standing held far greater importance than challenging the status quo.

So they let it go.

This kind of contradiction creates a dangerous gap between what leaders say they want and how they actually respond when confronted with uncomfortable truths. *"We want to hear from you,"* quickly turns into, *"We didn't expect to hear this,"* followed by the power to dismiss, reject, or even penalize those who spoke up. This erodes credibility and trust, sending a clear message: truth is welcome when it doesn't challenge our comfort, our image, or someone we're close to.

Leaders must be willing to confront not just the uncomfortable truths about themselves, but also about those they support and protect. In this case, the CEO's unwillingness to acknowledge her colleague's behavior and her complicity in harmful practices not only failed those who spoke up—it actively undermined the organization's mission and values. What ultimately failed was the organization's momentum in expanding its membership, including sizeable financial contributions that were withheld by members waiting to see if leadership would deliver on its words.

This was the moment the organization's mission was abandoned. They protected their comfort by dismissing difficult truths instead of embracing discomfort and becoming stronger from it.

2. CONTRADICTION OF IDENTITY

The second major threat to purpose is when a leader's self-perception contradicts how others experience them. Many leaders take pride in their reputation, but when faced with feedback that clashes with their self-image, they resist.

I worked with a leader who let his ego drive his choices, ultimately compromising a start-up company that held incredible promise. On the surface, he was an individual with a reputation for high integrity and strong values, liked by everyone. As the CEO, he held full decision-making power—not only because of his title but because he was deeply trusted and respected, particularly by those with less experience in the business world. This trust led to unquestioned authority over financial decisions, enabling him to operate without oversight, placing the company in considerable debt.

Despite repeated requests for financial reports from the largest investor, he viewed these inquiries as suggestions. For nearly two years, instead of providing any P/L reports, he deflected by offering plausible-sounding explanations that appeared cooperative but were carefully crafted to avoid accountability and maintain control.

When a more seasoned operations executive joined the company and conducted a SWOT analysis paired with a data-driven ROI strategy, it wasn't seen as an opportunity for growth. Instead, the CEO perceived it as a threat. It revealed long-ignored gaps in performance and exposed the lack of foundational data analytics within the organization. He resented the incoming executive's proposal for stronger financial controls, transparency, and board-level accountability.

Ironically, the company's largest investor and co-founder who championed these changes was also the one bringing forward innovative ideas and strategies to strengthen the company. Yet, his voice was deliberately dismissed not because his ideas lacked merit but because they threatened the CEO's control. Behind closed doors, the CEO repeatedly discredited him, speaking negatively to colleagues and trusted contacts.

He spread falsehoods, sabotaged, and suppressed key information to shield himself from the fear that his own inexperience at this level was being exposed. As co-founder with a vested interest in the company's success, he only stood to benefit from advancing it into a sustainable enterprise but in these key moments where he held power without accountability, his instinct for self-protection blinded him to long-term gain.

The few who knew the truth were either sidelined or chose to remain silent, constrained by longstanding relationships and unspoken loyalties. Loyalty, in this case, didn't safeguard integrity—it protected dysfunction. As a result, the company remained stagnant.

This leader's story is a striking illustration that leadership can be deceiving when circumstances are easy and public. True character is not revealed when everything is easy. It's revealed when control, reputation, or power feel threatened.

This was the moment that stopped the company from evolving into a thriving enterprise. Instead of leveraging information to shape a strategic roadmap, he chose to protect perception over progress.

3. INEQUITY BEING EXPOSED

The third major threat to leadership purpose is when inequity is exposed—particularly favoritism disguised as merit. Many leaders unknowingly allow social dynamics, biases, and personal loyalties to dictate access to opportunities, promotions, and resources.

When inequity is exposed, it is often seen as a threat to the company, placing it in legal and reputational jeopardy. But what leaders generally fail to recognize is the report of inequity isn't the real threat—it's merely bringing to the surface what is already a widespread belief across the organization. Ignoring it doesn't make it disappear; it only reinforces a culture where distrust, favoritism, and exclusion thrive.

I helped an organization where favoritism was rampant, ingrained so deeply into the culture that it became normalized. Younger, more attractive employees were fast-tracked for promotions, advancing ahead of others with comparable or stronger performance. Older workers, some of whom had been loyal contributors for decades, were systematically laid off, separated, or terminated. The "golden" employees, those deemed the heirs apparent to executive leadership roles, were rewarded with invitations into key, visible projects and opportunities despite errors in their work, missed deadlines, and selective collaboration. Their success was based not on merit, but on how they looked, dressed, and acted. In this organization, your relationship with key executives determined your access, your opportunities, your influence, and ultimately whether you would rise or fall.

Meanwhile, highly talented employees who contributed significantly to their departments were overshadowed and overlooked. Their ideas were ignored, their performance dismissed, and their potential stifled simply because they didn't fit the mold of the "ideal" leader. Even HR was complicit, perpetuating this culture by selectively informing favored employees of new job openings and promotional opportunities while withholding this information from others. It was a closed circle of favoritism that excluded many while elevating a select few. This is what inequity actually looks like in practice.

The result was deeply damaging. Employees who had once admired the executive leadership team and the organization became disillusioned. They saw through the lip service of leaders who spoke about authenticity and innovation but whose actions betrayed their words. The highly dedicated and talented employees, disheartened by the insincerity of the company values, began to leave. They found opportunities elsewhere, taking their skills and loyalty with them. The company they once loved had lost its most valuable resource.

Favoritism breeds a toxic culture that divides teams, creating an environment where some employees are marginalized while others are undeservingly favored. Those who understood how to win favor with leadership knew how to act in front of the right people, while privately complaining to those willing to speak up. This strategic self-preservation deepened distrust, forcing employees to choose between staying silent to help themselves or speaking up and jeopardizing their standing.

Leaders who tolerate or perpetuate favoritism are not leading with purpose. Instead, they are fostering an environment where favorable bias overshadows talent, and personal loyalty takes precedence over performance.

This was the moment that blocked significant revenue potential. Rather than expanding their lens and being receptive to different talent, they upheld practices that aligned with the preferences of those already in power—prioritizing comfort over growth.

THE BIRTH OF THE TRANSFORMATION FORMULA

Through my research, I uncovered a defining difference between the 90% of purpose-driven leaders who falter when threats trigger the ego and threaten purpose—and the 10% who remain unshaken. It was by studying this rare 10% that I developed the **Transformation Formula**—a groundbreaking playbook that reveals how these leaders consistently stay aligned with their highest self and deepest purpose, even in the face of risk, resistance, or uncertainty. This framework is a behavioral blueprint for leading with purpose over ego, truth over comfort, and influence that leaves a legacy.

This isn't just another leadership model. The Transformation Formula isn't a theory. It's the answer to a question that has stalled meaningful progress even in the most well-intentioned organizations: **Why do so many change efforts fail—and what must happen to break that cycle?**

This framework was born from over 10 years of direct work with executive leaders behind closed doors. It introduces four distinct archetypes of purpose-driven leaders, each shaped by their relationship to pressure, purpose and principles. These archetypes are not theoretical constructs; they emerged through a thorough analysis of real behaviors, real decisions, and real consequences. While 90% fall into the first three archetypes—despite their good intentions, the rare 10% do something profoundly different.

They uphold their mission when it's most needed. They don't let fear, ego, or external forces dictate their interactions or choices.

This formula doesn't examine why *average* leaders fail. It focuses on those at their peak—respected, mission-driven, and influential—who, in key moments, chose self-preservation over purpose. It doesn't just show *where* they fell short. It reveals *why*: the hidden forces that caused them to fail others and themselves.

This is what gave rise to the Transformation Formula, anchored by the **5x5 Model**: the behavior-based companion for identifying the five derailers that cause leaders to abandon their purpose and the five gateway behaviors that return them to it. It ensures that your leadership is more than just words on a wall, but truly transformative.

1

THE TRUTH ABOUT POWER

Before we dive into the Transformation Formula, we have to confront something foundational: *Power.* How it's accessed. How it's acquired. But most importantly—how it's used. Because whether you realize it or not, every act of leadership is an act of power.

Power is the invisible current that runs beneath every choice, every conversation, every decision a leader makes. It determines whose voice gets heard, which priorities get funded, and what kind of culture silently forms in the spaces between what's said and what's left unsaid.

Leadership is power.

That statement alone may stir discomfort. We've been taught to associate power with ego, dominance, or manipulation—something to tiptoe around rather than claim. But at its core, power is simply this:

Power is the ability to influence decisions and impact outcomes that shape the experiences of others.

The moment you step into leadership, you step into power. You may not feel it. You may even reject the label. But power doesn't require your permission; it operates through your presence. In every meeting, every decision, every conversation, your power is at play. The only question is: how are you using it?

Are you aware of the impact your choices have on the people around you? Or are you vigilant about survival—avoiding risk, staying liked, staying safe—that you're unknowingly misusing or neglecting the very influence you've been entrusted with?

When I began working with executives and leadership teams navigating conflict, crisis, or cultural stagnation, I started to see the same pattern play out across industries and personalities. It wasn't just a strategy problem or a communication issue; it was a relationship problem. Not between people, but between leaders and their own power.

We are far more attuned to moments when we feel powerless than we are to the subtle ways we wield power daily. That unawareness doesn't protect us—it risks misuse. Even well-intentioned leaders fall into this trap.

Leadership isn't defined by inspiration. It's defined by decision.

And this realization led me to a critical insight: *Most leadership definitions are romanticized.* They sound inspiring but leave out the pressure. They speak of vision and values but ignore the tradeoffs and sacrifices. True leadership isn't about charisma or clever mission statements; it's about your relationship with power, especially when your comfort, reputation, or authority is on the line.

And those decisions often take place at the crossroads between what serves people and what serves protection.

So I began defining leadership in a new way. Not through a lens of aspiration, but responsibility.

Leaders are the seekers of truth, in pursuit of a greater purpose to make a meaningful difference. They carry both the privilege and the burden of decisions where elevating one priority requires sacrificing another. Their choices shape lives, impact businesses, and influence humanity's progress.

Leadership is inseparable from power and how that power is exercised in pivotal moments determines whether stagnation prevails or transformation takes root.

The way leaders engage with truth, especially when it challenges them, dictates whether they perpetuate the status quo or ignite meaningful change within individuals, organizations, and society at large.

And nothing reveals who a leader is more clearly than how they respond to truth.

THE POWER OF TRUTH

In virtually every environment where change failed, one variable stood out: Power and truth were at odds.

In theory, leaders say they want information, insights, and feedback. This is what truth is. But, in practice, this truth, when it's unfavorable, is dismissed, especially when it disrupts comfort, threatens authority, or exposes what's not working. Because truth is treated as a threat. A destabilizer. A liability. Instead of being embraced as insights to consider, it's seen as a confrontation.

But what if we redefined truth? What if we stopped viewing truth as an attack or as a weapon and started seeing it as a form of intelligence? Rather than seeking to dispute its validity, we treated it as a critical data point for consideration? What if discomfort or resistance was no longer the reason to retreat, but a signal to pay closer attention?

Real change cannot take form in environments where truth is suppressed. Truth has the power to completely shut down change or be the complete breakthrough for change. Truth isn't the enemy. It is *the* breakthrough.

Here's what I've learned first-hand: A remarkable shift happens when a leader redefines their relationship with truth. Absolutely everything changes. I've seen it happen in the middle of strategy sessions, conflict resolutions, and executive retreats. One person speaks an unspoken reality aloud. The air changes. A room exhales. Honesty becomes oxygen.

As truth unfolds and gets tackled, an undeniable intimacy forms that becomes both instant and profound. It's that palpable. It's incredible to witness, even more powerful to experience. From that moment, trust begins to build. Not because people agree, but because they finally feel safe enough to tell the truth. Suddenly, the conversation isn't performative—it's real. Vulnerable. Alive.

If transformation is the destination, then truth is the road that gets us there. But only if leaders are willing to take it.

When truth is presented, it becomes a defining moment and that's what makes it pivotal.

WHAT HAPPENS WHEN POWER FEELS THREATENED

Here's where it gets complicated. If truth is the path to transformation, why don't more leaders embrace it?

Because telling or receiving the truth often activates the most primal instinct in leadership: **self-preservation**. Across my work with senior leaders, I've identified three distinct threats that trigger this reflex. These moments may look subtle from the outside, but they activate powerful internal alarms:

Threat to position—*fear of losing title, income, or rank.*

When a leader feels their position is threatened—whether by organizational shifts, competing talent, or internal politics—this leads to alignment with the status quo. Sustaining one's livelihood, although a valid concern, can cause them to align with harmful decisions, engage in silencing dissent, or avoid risk to ensure continued employment and income. The perceived threat to position triggers decisions aimed at survival, not transformation.

Threat to power—*fear of losing control, privilege, or access.*

Power is safety. It offers more than authority. It provides access, influence, protection, and the ability to shape outcomes. Over time, it can quietly become something a leader depends on to feel worthy, significant, or untouchable. When that power is challenged—through shifting dynamics, empowered voices, or demands for accountability—a leader may begin to grip harder. In response, they may withhold information, invalidate input, or override collaboration to tighten decisions and maintain the upper hand. The threat lies not in losing a title, but in losing the advantages power includes.

Threat to favor—*fear of losing political capital, social currency, or positive standing with key influencers.*

Favor is the quiet currency of belonging. It governs access to opportunity, stability, advancement, and perceived value. When an individual senses they're at risk of falling out of favor—with executives, friends, or key decision-makers—they may begin to protect their favor at all costs.

This threat taps into something deeper than politics; it touches identity, worthiness, and the need for inclusion. To stay aligned with those with power, leaders may abandon what they believe, stay silent in the face of wrongdoing, or distance themselves from those doing what's right.

These threats don't scream—they whisper. It's a gut feeling. A moment of doubt. A subtle pull to stay quiet, to align with what's safe, to distance yourself from someone telling the truth because their candor feels too risky to stand beside.

And just like that, your power is no longer in service of your purpose, it's in service of your protection.

Every leader will face these crossroads. But not every leader will recognize them. And that's the danger. If unexamined, these moments become the reasons transformation never takes hold.

The greatest barriers to transformative leadership aren't external—they're internal. It's the quiet, unseen battle between self-preservation and purpose.

WHERE POLITICS BEGIN AND CULTURE UNRAVELS

Unchecked self-preservation doesn't exist in a vacuum. Politics is the use of favorable currency. It's how access, protection, or influence get distributed, not necessarily based on value, but on loyalty or likeability.

Politics and power don't just influence a company's culture, they define it. The silent alliances, behind-the-scenes positioning, unspoken favors, and protective loyalties that emerge in a setting don't happen by accident. They are the inevitable result when power becomes a game of access, currency, and optics rather than a tool of purpose, principle, and truth.

When politics dominate, power is no longer exercised to serve the mission, it's used to secure proximity, protect reputation, or manipulate perception. And when that becomes the unspoken norm, culture suffers. Not just morale. But innovation. Inclusion. Performance.

And yet, political behavior often goes unchecked, not because it's invisible, but because it's embedded into "how things are done" and "it's easier." When politics go unexamined, culture becomes contaminated by favoritism, fear, and survival tactics masquerading as strategy.

If you're leading in a culture where people avoid conflict, hoard information, or trade loyalty for access, you're not just leading through politics, you're reinforcing them.

If politics are involved, you have an unhealthy culture. And if you have an unhealthy culture, your business hasn't reached its full potential. Even if it's performing well, it still hasn't become what it's capable of. It's that simple.

POLITICS VS. PERFORMANCE

But let's draw an important line. Not every visible or influential team member is playing politics. One of the most dangerous blind spots employees can have is mislabeling high performance as political behavior. Because politics are so prevalent in many organizations, it becomes easy to project those dynamics onto people who are simply showing up with skill, value, and availability.

Sometimes what's perceived as "favoritism" is actually a recognition of consistent excellence.

Certain individuals stand out because they're reliable, solutions-oriented, and clear in how they think and communicate. They're accessible, follow through, and back up their ideas with sound reasoning and real results. They bring emotional intelligence into challenging conversations.

Rewarding these individuals is not a result of special treatment or politics. They are being rewarded for their excellence.

And it's a mistake to discredit high performers' contributions by categorizing their influence as politics. We must be careful not to label someone's visibility or impact as manipulation simply because they've done the work to lead well.

At the same time, the difference between performance and politics depends on whether opportunities to influence are equitably distributed. If you, as a leader, only make space for certain people to be heard—those who align with your preferences or those who are always visible or always agreeable—you may unintentionally be creating a political environment where access, not ability, determines who gets to shape decisions.

It's not political when someone chooses to be available, prepared, and ready to contribute.

It *is* political when others aren't given the opportunity to do the same.

So the responsibility goes both ways:

- As a leader, you must actively examine who you listen to, who you seek out, and who you allow to influence you.
- As a team member, you must be honest with yourself: Are you contributing value? Are you stepping up with ideas and solutions? Or are you standing back and assuming that visibility equals favoritism?

When you misunderstand power, mislabel performance, or fail to examine your own role in how influence is distributed, you're not just misreading your team, you're shaping a culture that rewards optics over impact. Unchecked assumptions distort reality. They create resistance where none is warranted. Individuals who don't challenge their perceptions risk discrediting the very people who are driving results. And teams that don't examine their biases may resist influence not because it's political but because it challenges them to grow.

In transformation work, this level of clarity is imperative. Knowing the difference between politics and performance is essential to building a culture where real influence—earned influence—is not only possible but demonstrable.

THE CROSSROADS OF LEADERSHIP

Behind the curtain, I've witnessed leaders whom I've deeply respected—some of the most capable and purpose-driven individuals—confront moments that quietly test everything they stand for. These aren't dramatic events, and they rarely come with warning signs. They're subtle. They unfold in private exchanges: a decision that risks disappointing a powerful stakeholder, a conversation with a close colleague that might ignite conflict, or a moment when silence feels safer than the truth.

It's in these moments that leadership is stripped of its title and exposed for what it really is: a choice between conviction and convenience.

At this intersection, a leader faces an internal reckoning. It arrives in the form of discomfort: when truth begins to challenge loyalty, when speaking up might disrupt the fragile harmony of a relationship, or when dismantling norms threatens to shift power away from where it's long been concentrated. These quiet tensions—between purpose and ego—are what I've come to call the ***crossroads of leadership.***

You've likely stood at a crossroads like this. But if you haven't yet, you will. Not once, but many times. The higher you rise, the greater the stakes. The more influence you carry, the more frequently you'll be faced with decisions that test your alignment, your integrity, and your impact. The choices you make at this crossroads will shape your reputation, define your legacy, and ultimately determine the kind of leader you become.

I've seen these crossroads repeatedly separate those who belong to the 90%—leaders who abandon their purpose under this pressure—from the rare 10% who remain grounded when it was most needed and the most difficult to do. Every one of these inflection points is triggered by a truth that is difficult to face. The pressure to protect oneself is immense. And the path of least resistance, the one with the fewest consequences and the least friction in the short term, is almost always the one that quietly pulls a leader away from their highest self and their highest potential.

If unrecognized and unmanaged, these moments will undermine your credibility and define your leadership in ways you never intended. But when met with clarity and courage, these same moments become something else entirely: A proving ground for transformation. A moment that shapes not just what you do, but who you are as a leader.

WHERE YOUR REAL POWER LIVES

Here's what I want you to know as you step into this book: Even when you feel powerless, you're not. Even when systems seem blocked, people are resistant, or politics are present, you still have power. You may not have the social currency. You may not have an equal allocation of budget. Or, it may not be in your title. But it lives in three places no one can take from you.

- **Choice** – No one can take away your ability to decide how you show up in your role, if you contribute or coast. You're not a victim of circumstance, no matter the mountain in front of you. You have the power of choice.
- **Character** – No one can take away your ability to choose who you are, your integrity, or your principles in any situation, no matter what power is in the room. The conviction of your character is power.
- **Competence** – No one can take away the knowledge, skills, and experience you've developed. What you bring to the table can shape conversations, influence decisions, and drive meaningful impact. Your expertise is your source of power.

It's a fascinating phenomenon—how many people who hold power yet feel powerless in their influence. The dynamics within teams, politics, and relationships often silence even those at the top.

I've seen executives, senior leaders, and decision-makers hesitate, question their influence, or shrink in key moments. That's why I want you to know this: even in moments when you feel powerless, you still hold power. Always. It lives in those three fundamental areas, each one already within you, ready to be called on when needed.

Power is relational, emotional, and behavioral. The question isn't, *"Do I have it?"* Ask instead: *"How am I using it, and am I aware of the impact I have?"*

Are you leveraging it to create change, challenge stagnation, and lead with truth? Or are you rationalizing your self-preservation to quietly legitimize your actions?

These questions aren't meant to criticize but to encourage deep reflection in your private moments with yourself. Consider them an invitation to step fully into your power, not shy away from it. When you begin to notice where your power lives, you also begin to notice where you've been giving it away—or misusing it without realizing it.

And when you meet resistance, don't retreat. Resistance is often the very feedback you need. Resistance is often your greatest source of insight. It's not a dead end—it's a directional cue. It shows you what needs to shift, not in your worth, but in your delivery. It's not a signal to stop; it's a sign to refine. In my work, I've seen it time and again: the opinion or input has the right intent but the method needs refinement. The positioning isn't persuasive because it's missing key elements. Influence isn't about pushing harder and it isn't about informing. It's about becoming more precise in how, when, and where you lead others to listen. It's knowing how to reach people in a way they can actually receive.

THIS IS WHERE IT BEGINS

What I'm sharing with you about transformative leadership is grounded in practice and results. It's how transformation really happens at the moment where purpose meets protection and leaders must decide what matters more.

You may never feel completely ready. You may never feel fully safe. But you are not ever completely powerless.

You hold more influence than you think. And you have everything you need to lead with truth, purpose, and impact—right now.

This is where your transformation begins. Let's begin it together.

Be unshaken—not by resisting change,
but by anchoring your choices in truth so deeply
that no tide can move you. In doing so, you don't just
withstand the storm—you calm it for others.

2

WHAT SEPARATES THE 10%

Some of the most brilliant, passionate, and committed leaders I've worked with have also been the ones who faltered when their leadership was needed most. They weren't lacking purpose. They had vision. They had integrity. They were genuinely committed to doing good or doing better.

And yet, when they stood at the crossroads between ego and purpose, 90% of purpose-driven leaders let ego lead.

That became the foundation of my work. I focused on purpose-driven leaders; not because they were failing, but because they were trying. They had inspiring visions, genuine commitment, and the desire to champion change. These were not passive players. They didn't lack intelligence, charisma, or influence. If anything, their purpose is what drove their ambitions and motivations.

But purpose wasn't enough.

So what separates the 10% who remain unshaken at that crossroads? That question became the catalyst for developing the **Transformation Formula**. I needed to go beyond surface-level insight into why purpose-driven leaders falter. I needed to trace the abandonment back to its origin. What enables the 10% to stay grounded when everything was on the line? When doing so may damage their image, their standing with those in power, or jeopardize their own security? The 10% are willing to make a decision that betters the business, tackle the truth before it becomes an employment lawsuit, and repair a fractured team. The result? They get more out of their teams and outperform their counterparts who are too focused on perceptions.

So, how do they override the impulse to self-protect? How do they choose the company's mission when politics would be easier? The answer wasn't fearlessness. It wasn't more integrity, stronger character, or greater humility. The difference lies in something more profound: **principles.**

THE POWER OF PRINCIPLES

Leaders in the 10% live and lead by a set of unwavering principles: nonnegotiable commitments that amplify their purpose when their comfort, reputation, or security is on the line.

They don't just believe in a mission greater than themselves. They *act* in alignment with that mission even if means jeopardizing what they value personally. For these leaders, principles act as a stabilizing force. They allow leaders to say hard things, make unpopular decisions, and speak truth even when silence would be easier and safer. They don't just inspire others, they lead with congruence and credibility.

Purpose may spark belief, but only principles make it believable.

Principles are the code you will not abandon,
no matter the risk or sacrifice, in service to
the higher mission or greater good.

When a leader operates from a deep sense of purpose and anchors that purpose in nonnegotiable principles, they create the conditions for transformation—not just for themselves, but for their teams, their organizations, and even society.

This is the sweet spot. The intersection where inspiration meets action. High-purpose, high-principle leadership fosters trust, drives innovation, and ignites change that lasts.

For the 10%, principles are more than ideals. They are lived standards, an unshakable code that holds them up under the pressure to protect themselves and serve the collective good when conditions need to improve.

A LESSON FROM JOHN WICK 4

What's the difference between principles and values?

Consider a scene from *John Wick: Chapter 4*. John realizes he is bringing the vengeance of the High Table down on Koji's Continental in Osaka, and he apologizes to his friend for the trouble he has caused. His friend Shimazu says, "Friendship means little when it's convenient."

After saying this, Shimazu remains by John's side, demonstrating his commitment to their friendship despite the personal risk involved. The value here is friendship, and the principle is how Shimazu upholds that friendship by standing by John, especially when there's a threat to his own safety.

For all of us committed to leading with a strong sense of purpose and making a difference, we must understand this. Purpose means little when it's convenient. When our purpose is challenged, will we stay true to it, or will we divert and abandon it?

This is where many leaders get confused. They mistake values for principles. But here's the distinction:

- **Values** are what we believe in and aspire to.
- **Principles** are the behavioral commitments we uphold even when it costs us something to do so.

Values guide identity. Principles govern behavior. Purpose shapes impact.

And yet, the industry of leadership development has overindulged in what feels good—values and purpose—without doing the hard work of what holds it all together: principles. This is where the real gap lies.

When we can choose, do we choose chocolate or broccoli?

CHOCOLATE OR BROCCOLI? WHY POSITIVE PSYCHOLOGY ISN'T ENOUGH

I'll be honest—I hate broccoli, which is why I chose it for this analogy. And I love chocolate, so that's my choice of dessert. But depending on your personal preferences, feel free to substitute your dessert versus vegetables. Maybe for you, it's McDonald's french fries versus mushrooms. (Okay, those are mine too.) The point is, when it comes to leadership, we've built an entire field around what tastes good, feels good, and sells easily . . . and we've avoided the stuff that's harder to swallow.

Over the past decade, leadership development has become synonymous with the language and practices of positive psychology. Introduced by Martin Seligman and Mihaly Csikszentmihalyi, cofounders of Positive Psychology, it quickly gained traction because of its optimistic focus: human flourishing, meaning, strengths, engagement, quality social connections, and well-being. It aligned perfectly with what organizations wanted to hear . . . and what leaders wanted to feel. It gave rise to strength-based assessments, visioning tools, gratitude practices, optimism training, and frameworks for "leading with purpose."

And it sells. We do need this and I'm not saying this to dilute its importance or need. My point is: it is incomplete. Drawing upon positive psychology is only paying attention to half of who we are as humans.

Purpose inspires. Gratitude invigorates. Emotional intelligence ignites. Programs centered around empathy and strengths-based development fill quickly. Models that focus on hope, values, and high engagement are seen as progressive and safe.

These are the things that make a leader feel good about who they are and what they stand for. It's leadership as inspiration. Identity. Aspiration.

In other words: it's dessert.

Dessert is craved. It's in demand. It doesn't challenge the leader too much. And because it feels good, it became the dominant paradigm.

But in centering only the bright side of leadership, we've ignored the other half of the equation.

Yes, we've taught leaders to lead with purpose. But, this is how it's incomplete:

- We've taught purpose as inherently virtuous, without asking how easily it can be mistaken for optics or self-preservation.
- We haven't taught leaders how to examine when power shows up and when purpose is challenged.
- And we certainly haven't taught leaders to stay principled when it costs them something.

That's the missing half of the equation.

We've helped leaders conquer the shadows in other aspects of leadership, but not the shadows inherent in their power.

We've created a generation of leaders who are self-aware, empathetic, and purpose driven but who often cannot see when they are suppressing, controlling, or protecting themselves *at the expense of others.*

This is where the shadow lives. In the subtle moments when a leader prioritizes image over impact, comfort over conflict, or loyalty over truth. And we've left leaders unequipped to navigate it, because that work doesn't sell.

The dark side of leadership isn't marketable. It's not a six-week cohort with a workbook and a ribbon. It's introspective. Confrontational. Tough. It requires discipline, diving deep, and behavioral integrity—not surface level affirmation.

This is the **broccoli**. And this is where **principles** live.

Principles are not aspirational. They are behavioral. They don't make you feel good. As I'm writing this they don't even sound fun, and they definitely aren't enticing.

But . . . they make you unquestionably trustworthy. They are what govern your decisions when no one is watching, when your ego is triggered, and when protecting yourself would be easier than protecting the people you lead. This isn't about doing what they want, it's about doing what's right when the conditions aren't right.

We've trained leaders to know what they value. We haven't trained them to recognize when they're violating those values in real time. We haven't trained them to identify the moment power starts distorting purpose. And so:

- The same leader who champions collaboration will still make unilateral decisions.
- The one who says they value inclusion will still marginalize people that challenge them.

- The one who speaks of humility will still protect their image rather than admit fault.

It's not hypocrisy. Often, it's a lack of principle. They've been taught the language of leadership but not the discipline of it.

Consider a company that names collaboration as a core value. It's printed in onboarding decks, spoken of in team meetings, and included in quarterly goals. But senior leadership still excludes key stakeholders in key decisions. Impacted individuals are brought in too late to contribute meaningfully. Decisions are made, not shared. Collaboration is proclaimed but not practiced.

Why? Because the principle of shared decision-making was never defined, let alone upheld. The value is advertised, but the behavior isn't enforced. And slowly, the culture begins to rot from the inside out—not because people didn't care, but because no one was willing to hold the line when it became inconvenient.

This is what happens when we only serve dessert, only buy dessert, and only eat dessert. But now, it's time to invest in broccoli and the rest of our vegetables—the things that sustain us. They're what keep us healthy and thriving. Then, we can truly savor that chocolate cake even more.

If we want leaders to build trust, create safety, and drive transformation, they must be taught to *lead through power, not just purpose*. They must learn to recognize their derailers, name their principles, and align their behavior when no one is holding them accountable except themselves.

Principles keep **purpose** in the driver's seat and **ego** in the back seat, especially in moments when stability feels uncertain or threatened.

Transformation doesn't happen in the spotlight. It happens in the moments where your values are on the line and you choose not to abandon them.

We now know that purpose-driven leaders have not been equipped to fully understand, examine, or steward their power. Through my research, I uncovered four distinct archetypes of purpose-driven leaders—patterns that reveal *how leaders respond when their purpose is tested* and *how they wield power in moments that become pivotal when truth enters the equation.*

Before I introduce those archetypes, it's important to confront a common misconception. We all carry a mental image of who holds power. We associate it with gender, race, culture, and age. And while those associations often reflect systemic realities, I found something deeper. Demographics were not a predictor of which leaders upheld their purpose, championed change, or protected others from harm. The defining factor wasn't identity; it was proximity to power. No matter the race, gender, sexual orientation, or background, once a person held power, their relationship to that power—not their demographic—determined whether they led with principle or self-preservation. So if you have a picture in your mind of who falls into the 90% versus the 10%, check that image. Because power, not identity, was the great revealer—and no one was immune to it.

Each archetype begins with the highest of best intentions. But only one leads to true transformation.

THE 4 ARCHETYPES OF PURPOSE-DRIVEN LEADERSHIP

ARCHETYPE 1: PURPOSE-DRIVEN LEADERS EXPERIENCED AS **PERFORMATIVE**

Words Without Actions

These leaders speak passionately about values and inspire with vision, but they lack follow-through. They prioritize positivity over substance and optics over action. High on purpose, low on principles, they retreat when pressure threatens their image.

ARCHETYPE 2: PURPOSE-DRIVEN LEADERS EXPERIENCED AS **JUDGMENTAL**

Ideals Without Inspiration

These leaders hold tightly to high standards and convictions but lead with criticism rather than connection. Their principles are high, but their purpose isn't felt—resulting in a style that alienates rather than inspires.

ARCHETYPE 3: PURPOSE-DRIVEN LEADERS EXPERIENCED AS **OPPRESSIVE**

Harmony Over Truth

Experienced as kind, calm, or collaborative, these leaders avoid discomfort at all costs. Their preference for peace silences truth and protects comfort. In preserving their own stability, they bury their purpose and operate without guiding principles.

ARCHETYPE 4: PURPOSE-DRIVEN LEADERS EXPERIENCED AS **TRANSFORMATIVE**

Transparency of Truth

These are the rare 10% who stay true to the mission, even when it jeopardizes their stability. They embrace resistance, confront hard truths, and use tension as a catalyst for change. Purpose wins because their principles never waver.

Each archetype represents a distinct approach to purpose-driven leadership and reveals how purpose and principles are or aren't working together in practice. Understanding if your purpose is high or low, and if your principles are high or low, will help you to reflect on the gap between how you see yourself and how others experience your leadership.

HOW THE IMBALANCE OF PURPOSE OR PRINCIPLES SUSTAINS HARM

When leaders operate from self-protection, they push their purpose into the backseat—and principles aren't even in the car. They create environments that, whether intentionally or not, allow harm to persist.

Oppression in leadership doesn't look like ruthless decision-making or overt power plays. In fact, the most dangerous kind can be the hardest to recognize. It hides behind empathy, diplomacy, and a desire to "keep the peace." It speaks in reassuring tones, maintains harmony on the surface, and avoids disruption—even when disruption is exactly what's needed. This form of leadership manifests not as cruelty, but as complacency, conflict aversion, and an unconscious allegiance to the status quo.

I worked with an executive who embodied this dynamic. She reported directly to a CEO whose company was founded on inclusion and leadership excellence, yet behind closed doors the culture told a different story. Employees were being bullied, underpaid, and stretched beyond respectful limits, while unethical behavior was expected as loyalty to the company. She had the favor, the security, and the position to take a stand. Instead, she stayed surface level and chose personal stability (her generous salary, her relaxed responsibilities, and low stress) over true intervention. When the harm was addressed, she quit.

This is how harm perpetuates; not by malicious individuals making overtly harmful choices, but by well-intentioned leaders making choices for self at the expense of others.

Here's an invitation: Don't just define your purpose and definitely don't rely exclusively on your purpose. Anchor it in principles. Make it real. When it's costly. When it's lonely. When your role and the universal, collective good necessitates it.

If you want to create true change, if you want the competitive edge, if you want to lead from the front, your purpose must be more than a belief. It must be *backed by behavior*. And that behavior must be anchored in principle.

That is the only way to lead without compromise. That is how transformation begins.

WHY TRANSFORMATION MATTERS NOW MORE THAN EVER

We are living in an era of accelerated disruption. Technology is evolving faster than most organizations can absorb. Social expectations are reshaping workplace culture. Workforce demographics are evolving. What employees expect from leadership has fundamentally changed. Political polarization, economic instability, and global uncertainty are no longer occasional stressors, they're the norm. What once defined effective leadership—vision, strategy, execution—is being replaced by ambiguity, complexity, and the need for deeper human insight.

The leadership playbook we relied on for decades no longer applies in full. Familiar models of guidance, hierarchy, and certainty are breaking down, and in their place is a new reality—one that doesn't just test competence, but character.

This moment is more than a test; it's a turning point. It demands more than vision; it demands discernment. Because we want to shape a future that honors the complexity of our challenges and it must be led by those with the patience, aptitude, and principle to place the higher good at the center.

When faced with uncertainty or threat, the instinct to protect your role, your reputation, or your comfort will always be the path of least resistance, the more attractive route. But self-preservation is survival, not leadership.

The stakes have never been higher. The choices you make as leaders today will shape the future of our organizations, our communities, and our society. They transform not just businesses, but the people within them. And it begins with one simple but profound step: knowing where you stand today so you can step into the leader you are meant to be tomorrow.

CHOOSING THE RIGHT PATH

Transformative leadership reveals a powerful truth: 90% of leaders fail to drive change not because they lack vision or purpose, but because they compromise their values when they are met with a crossroads like those I've previously outlined. The stakes are high and self-preservation takes over. Every leader faces pivotal moments where purpose is either reinforced or abandoned.

Choosing the right path when you come upon your own crossroads doesn't require perfection. It's about principles. Every leader will face a crossroads where discomfort, risk, or fear presses against what they say they believe. The questions are these:

- Am I willing to embrace discomfort, perceived threats, or conflict in service of a greater purpose?
- When faced with a decision that could compromise the greater mission, do I choose what's right or what's comfortable?

Your answers will define your legacy.

Remember, your reputation as a leader is not just
built in public; it's shaped behind closed doors,
in those moments when only you hold the power
and choice to decide. It's in these private decisions
that you define your true character.

3

THE PURPOSE-DRIVEN
LEADERSHIP ARCHETYPES

Transformation doesn't begin when circumstances are favorable. It begins at the breaking point—when truth enters the room and puts your leadership under pressure. When your influence is questioned. When your position feels unstable. When you're faced with a decision that could either serve the mission or protect yourself.

These are the moments that separate who you aspire to be from how you actually lead.

This chapter describes in depth three of the archetypes of purpose-driven leaders. These are not fixed personality types, but behavioral patterns that emerge when purpose is tested. These are the lived realities of leaders who believed themselves to be values-driven, until the cost of truth demanded more than their comfort or control could withstand. It's not about who you are on your best day. It's about who you become if you allow, fear, ego, or image management to start making decisions.

As we explored in the last chapter, most leaders don't fail because they lack purpose. They fail because they abandon it—privately, unconsciously, and often while appearing highly effective. These archetypes reveal how that happens, and more importantly, how to interrupt it.

Your task is not to diagnose others, no matter how tempting that might be. Let that be the second time you read this chapter. The first time, focus on locating yourself. Not on your best day, but in the moments when your character is under pressure—when something unpleasant, inconvenient, or unfavorable threatens your stability or control. This isn't about judgment. It's about honesty. Not in your intention, but in but how others experience you when your power feels unsteady. Because that's the moment transformation begins—not in how leadership appears, but in the decision to live who you want to be.

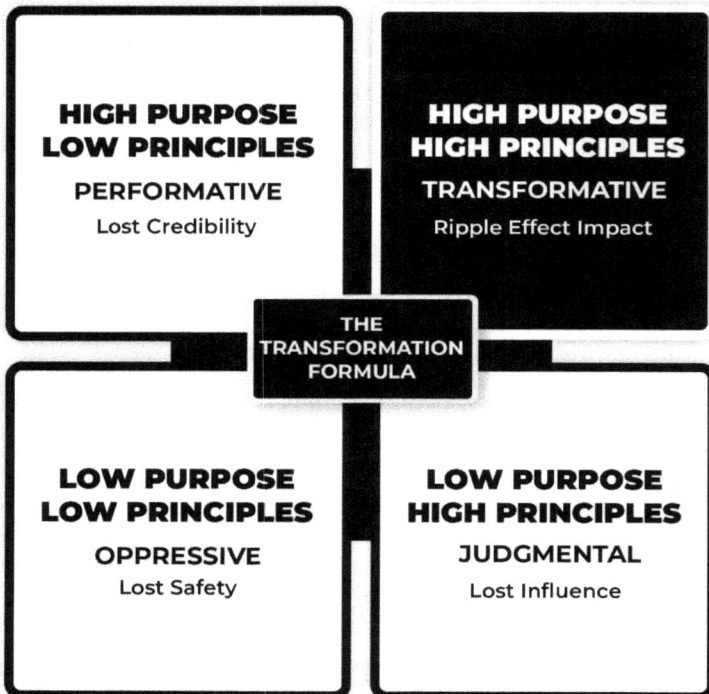

HIGH PURPOSE LOW PRINCIPLES

PERFORMATIVE

Lost Credibility

HIGH PURPOSE HIGH PRINCIPLES

TRANSFORMATIVE

Ripple Effect Impact

THE TRANSFORMATION FORMULA

LOW PURPOSE LOW PRINCIPLES

OPPRESSIVE

Lost Safety

LOW PURPOSE HIGH PRINCIPLES

JUDGMENTAL

Lost Influence

ARCHETYPE 1: PURPOSE-DRIVEN LEADERS WHO ARE PERFORMATIVE

High in Purpose, Low in Principles

Key phrase: *Inspire through words, fail in action*

Outcome: *Leaders lose credibility*

Purpose-driven leaders who are performative are sincere and charismatic. They radiate passion, speak with authenticity, and deeply care about making a difference. Their ability to cast a compelling vision and emotionally connect with others makes them powerful influencers. Teams rally behind them. Organizations often admire them. These leaders are known for their energy, optimism, and bold ambition to drive meaningful change.

They can be exceptional at inspiring belief—sparking hope, momentum, and unity across their teams. Their speeches resonate. Their presence uplifts. And their enthusiasm creates a sense of possibility that others want to follow.

When performative leaders are at their best, they create the emotional ignition that fuels engagement. But inspiration alone isn't enough.

INSPIRE THROUGH WORDS, FAIL IN ACTION

Despite their powerful beginnings, performative leaders struggle to stay grounded when pressure rises. Without clear principles to anchor them, they begin to avoid the work that is more complex, time-consuming, and harder to measure—the work that demands sustained effort, not just surface engagement.

They either overfocus on positivity or, when they do engage in harder conversations, they stay safely on the surface. They comfortably discuss operational metrics, budget forecasts, or revenue targets, but are unwilling to examine the cultural or interpersonal behaviors undermining progress.

Their leadership efforts center around activities that look productive, generate recognition, and maintain participation but don't actually challenge the deeper issues blocking real change. They celebrate momentum for completing initiatives, attending workshops, or launching DEI efforts, yet avoid evaluating whether these efforts are effective or aligned with the real problems.

Because their work stays externally focused and low risk, it never truly penetrates the layers where change lives. The moment risk enters—when tough choices, relational strain, or political risk show up—they pivot. They stop. They soften their stance. Or they abandon the effort altogether. That's the defining trait of this archetype: they act, but not accurately. They move, but not meaningfully. They begin with fire but end with silence.

I've seen this pattern repeatedly. Leaders who cast inspiring visions and create genuine excitement at the start but as resistance emerges, they back away. Instead of staying in the tension, they rationalize shortcuts, downplay friction, or prioritize the path of least resistance. They protect their comfort, their likability, and their position at the expense of the mission.

The problem isn't a lack of sincerity. Their conviction disappears when it's most needed.

Over time, the gap between their inspiring words and their misaligned actions becomes too large to ignore. Teams begin to feel not just disappointed—but disillusioned. And what once felt like leadership now reveals itself as superficial.

THE OUTCOME: LOSE CREDIBILITY

The greatest consequence with performative leadership is the inevitable erosion of a leader's credibility. It's a slow burn. At first, individuals notice small incongruences—but they extend the benefit of the doubt. The leader's authenticity buys time, and trust holds for a while. But as time passes, the lack of meaningful action—or the incongruence to which activities are prioritized—becomes too consistent to ignore. What began as quiet doubt becomes disappointment. That disappointment deepens into disbelief. Eventually, the leader's words no longer carry weight—not because the team has become cynical, but because they've been let down too many times. The loss isn't just trust in the message, it's trust in the messenger.

New employees often still believe—hopeful, idealistic, and untested by experience. But those who've been around longer know better. They've seen the promises. They've waited for the follow-through. And now, they don't just question the message—they've stopped expecting change altogether.

The deeper issue? Performative leaders don't realize they've lost credibility. They continue leading with the same passion and polished language, unaware the people around them have grown quiet because they've stopped expecting things to change. The respect they once felt has faded.

That's the cost of staying at the surface. You rarely see the moment trust is lost, but from that point on the momentum is also lost and progress stalls.

EXAMPLE

I coached a dynamic CEO who embodied this archetype. He was a visionary, brimming with passion and ideas that energized everyone around him. People admired his authenticity and praised his commitment to addressing social injustices, both in society and within the workplace. His ability to inspire made the entire workforce believe in a brighter, more inclusive future, and they were eager to follow him.

Over time, the sincerity of his values faded. His actions no longer matched his words. He played favorites, granting special treatment to those who fit a certain image, while holding others to inconsistent and often harsher standards. The company culture began to reflect his contradictions.

Promotions went to those who privately criticized leadership but strategically aligned themselves with influential figures. Meanwhile, colleagues who raised concerns were labeled as "non-team players," unsupported and penalized. In the shadows, whispers turned to murmurs of disappointment:

"I really believed in him. But he plays favorites. If you're not in his circle, you can feel it."

"I looked up to him. I thought he stood for something real. Turns out, it was all just for show."

Gradually, this inconsistency eroded the trust that once made his leadership so compelling. He inspired through words but failed in action, leaving his team caught between lofty ideals and an unfulfilled reality. As trust crumbled, talented team members walked away, seeking workplaces where words and actions aligned.

ARCHETYPE 1: HIGH PURPOSE, LOW PRINCIPLES

This archetype is **high** in **purpose** and **low** in **principles**.

The leader communicates a compelling mission. The vision is clear. The authenticity is real. But when that vision isn't reinforced through consistent, principled action, credibility and respect collapses.

Greatest strength: Their authenticity and passion. These leaders genuinely care, and their purpose is often contagious. They can unite and inspire others around a greater cause.

Greatest gap: Sustaining long-term respect and trust because their decisions and behaviors fail to align with their words.

How to break the pattern: This leader must strengthen their principles, which drive their ability to make difficult decisions that may disrupt harmony, invite criticism, or allow discomfort to exist. They must be willing to sacrifice positivity in service of truth and allow tension to be part of the process, trusting that transparency creates cohesion more than approval or applause.

ARCHETYPE 2: PURPOSE-DRIVEN LEADERS WHO ARE JUDGMENTAL

High in Principles, Low in Purpose
Key phrase: *Idealism lost in criticism*
Outcome: *Leaders lose influence*

Purpose-driven leaders who are judgmental are driven by an unwavering sense of justice, holding themselves and others to exceptionally high standards. They are deeply committed to their values. They have a strong internal compass and believe deeply in fairness, equity, and doing what's right—especially for those who are disadvantaged or overlooked. They advocate for the underdog, speak truth to power, and hold tightly to ideals that many others are willing to compromise. Their compass can be refreshing in environments clouded by ambiguity or politics.

They are the ones who ask hard questions when others stay silent. Their commitment to principle can act as a safeguard for integrity within the organization. Teams often appreciate their convictions and the sense of safety that comes from knowing where these leaders stand. They bring sharp insights and a deep desire to build something better rooted in ethics. However, criticism without any proposed resolution simply creates more issues.

IDEALISM LOST IN CRITICISM

Their principles are so strong that they overpower their purpose, drowning out inspiration and connection. Judgmental leaders focus on how things *should* be, but become increasingly disillusioned by how things actually are. They may speak in absolutes, and lead more by critique than by collaboration.

Their high standards become weapons instead of guiding stars. They're quick to identify what's wrong but slow to recognize what's possible. Over time, they begin to sit in their contempt, frustrated with others, skeptical of progress, and increasingly cynical about change. They may see themselves as the lone voice of truth, but fail to see how their tone, approach, or rigidity alienates those they are trying to influence or lead.

Instead of building momentum, they reinforce division. Their leadership becomes reactive—focused on what's missing, what's flawed, and what others have failed to do. Rather than unifying people around a shared vision, they sustain silos and foster separation.

The painful irony is this: they are upholding what is right but doing so in a way that others experience as punitive. Rather than fostering transformation, they create a culture of compliance.

THE OUTCOME: LOSE INFLUENCE

Without a compelling purpose to unify and uplift, judgmental leaders lose their ability to influence. They inform, but they don't persuade. They often fail to recognize that offering input or opinions is not the same as positioning insights to inspire action. They make points to be right, rather than to create progress. Over time, this fixation on being right turns into critique and self-centeredness. Although in their minds, it feels like advocacy for others.

Progress stalls—not because their ideas lack merit, but because their delivery repels rather than inspires. They maintain silos, deepen division, and ultimately stop the growth of the people and systems around them. Their commitment to principle remains intact, but their impact is diminished.

Principles give you conviction; purpose is what you express and communicate through.

I learned this early in my career in the early 2000s.

At the time, I believed I was leading with purpose, but in reality I was letting principles take the driver's seat. While leading culture change for a corporation of 35,000 employees, I was asked to write the company's message on inclusion on behalf of the chief human resources officer (CHRO). For the first time in my entire career—perhaps the only time—I felt a genuine desire to resist and decline. That alone was significant because I was always a "yes" person to anything asked of me. My hesitation wasn't rooted in defiance, but partly in naivete, and also deeply in conviction. My reasoning? I believed that if the message was coming from him, the words needed to come *from him*. If they were mine, stamped with his name and title, it felt dishonest. So I deflected.

At the time, I told myself that I was leading with purpose and that inclusion comes from the sincerity of one's heart. But in hindsight, my evasion was rooted in judgment, not purpose. Instead of seeing an opportunity to shape the conversation and influence the message, I let my judgment limit my ability to make an important impact.

Today, I operate differently. When asked to craft messages like this, I say yes—not because my principles have changed, but because I now understand that principles must serve purpose—they don't replace it.

Your principles are the standards you hold yourself to— guiding your own values and actions—rather than a measure by which you judge others.

ARCHETYPE 2: LOW PURPOSE, HIGH PRINCIPLES

This archetype is *high* in *principles* and *low* in *purpose*.

These leaders operate with unwavering conviction. They are committed to doing what's right and they uphold fairness, consistency, and structure with discipline. Their standards are high—for themselves and for others.

Greatest strength: Their conviction to do right by others. These leaders are seen as dependable, ethical, and principled. They have a clear internal compass and hold themselves accountable to it, regardless of external pressure.

Greatest gap: Their inability to unify and the patience to meet people where they are. They struggle to translate their high standards into a shared mission others can connect with.

How to break the pattern: They must lead with purpose instead of their principles. This leader must develop the skillset to influence—learning to position their insights strategically, persuade through purpose, and shift from making points to making progress. They must move beyond offering opinions or information and learn how to truly inspire action. By learning to articulate the deeper "why" behind their convictions, they can shift from enforcement to empowerment and drive change that inspires, rather than isolates.

ARCHETYPE 3: PURPOSE-DRIVEN LEADERS WHO ARE OPPRESSIVE

Low in Purpose, Low in Principles
Key phrase: *Dishonest harmony over truth*
Outcome: *Leaders impede safety*

Purpose-driven leaders who are oppressive are highly regarded. They have emotional sophistication and savviness in cultivating harmonious environments. They present as calm, diplomatic, and highly relational. They're praised for their ability to maintain team cohesion, avoid escalation, and keep themselves steady. Their strength lies in their composure, discretion, and exceptional ability to make others feel listened to and comfortable. They often occupy trusted positions because they know how to navigate personalities, mediate surface-level tensions, and avoid open conflict. On the surface, they appear balanced, gracious, and highly well-intentioned.

DISHONEST HARMONY OVER TRUTH

Purpose-driven leaders who are oppressive are often the most surprising archetype because they are difficult to spot. Their calm demeanor masks a deep instinct to keep things smooth even if it means silencing what is real. When unpleasant information surfaces, these leaders may deflect, reframe the issue entirely, or discredit the person or information brought forward, all in the spirit of preserving harmony.

They value the appearance of unity over the need for accountability. Rather than engage difficult truths, they seek to preserve emotional comfort—whether their own or to protect someone close to them. These aren't abrasive leaders; they don't dominate with force. They diminish in a quiet way.

Preservation, safety, or stability are in the driver's seat. In their effort to prevent tension, they create an environment where stagnation becomes acceptable. The paradox is striking: even with a deep and genuine desire for change, their reluctance to face discomfort becomes the very barrier that keeps transformation out of reach.

THE OUTCOME: IMPEDE SAFETY

The result is a culture that feels stable but suffocates growth. Teams become underutilized and undervalued. Feedback disappears. Innovation stalls. Trust erodes. Employees self-censor, disengage, or quietly leave. What's lost is not only psychological safety, but the full potential of the people and the mission.

These leaders don't just avoid conflict—they avoid disruption of the status quo. In protecting harmony, they protect dysfunction. And in doing so, they make safety conditional: you are only safe if you don't speak the truth.

EXAMPLE

I partnered with a mid-sized company led by an executive team that exemplified purpose-driven oppressive leadership. The CEO had inherited the family business and felt immense pressure to uphold its legacy. Her primary focus was on maintaining harmony. She prioritized keeping the peace even when it directly hindered the company's success.

One department, in particular, was consistently underperforming—missing deadlines, delivering subpar work, and causing friction with other teams. When I asked what was causing her to dismiss the concerns, she replied, *"I don't want to alienate them. They've been here since the company was founded."*

Rather than confronting the clear dysfunction, she subtly shifted the narrative, downplaying the department's failures and discrediting those who spoke up with statements like *"They always find something to complain about."*

Over time, those who raised concerns found themselves quietly excluded from key meetings and decisions. Their influence gradually eroded, but in a way that was so subtle and strategic, others didn't even notice until it was too late.

This quiet undermining created a culture of silence. Employees eventually learned that challenging the status quo came at a cost. Even when concerns were valid and necessary, speaking up meant being sidelined.

On the surface, the CEO remained kind and measured, but her unwillingness to address difficult truths perpetuated stagnation, eroded trust, and stifled any potential for real progress.

Her need for harmony over truth became the very thing that kept the company stagnant. By prioritizing comfort over personal ownership, she unknowingly protected dysfunction at the expense of progress. In trying to keep the peace, she was compromising the very future of the business.

ARCHETYPE 3: LOW PURPOSE, LOW PRINCIPLES

This archetype is *low* in *purpose* and *low* in *principles* because self-preservation is their highest priority. These leaders may appear steady, composed, and gracious on the surface, but their leadership is largely shaped by the desire to avoid personal instability or risk, often at the expense of others, truth, and progress.

Greatest strength: Their presence brings calm and harmony. They bring a grounding energy to their teams. They reduce interpersonal tension, maintain stability, and are seen as approachable, empathetic, and even keeled.

Greatest gap: To confront the unspoken because their avoidance becomes a liability. They can deflect, discredit, or dismiss the dysfunctions, inefficiencies, and vulnerabilities that hold the organization back.

How to break the pattern: At the core, both purpose and principles must be cultivated and activated. While these leaders speak in the language of *we*, when tension rises their actions quietly center on *me*. They express empathy, but it doesn't translate into courageous action when the responsibility or ownership falls on them. And that's where the work begins.

To lead differently, they must build a deeper connection to a purpose beyond themselves and make a conscious commitment to principles in action so when the crossroads appear, it is *service to the greater mission*, not self-preservation, that drives their decisions.

SELF-AWARENESS

No leader operates above their own blind spots. Even the most committed can find themselves making decisions that, upon reflection, don't fully align with their purpose. The difference between stagnation and transformation is the ability to recognize when you're stuck and shift back to your higher purpose before misalignment turns into dysfunction.

Leaders often hesitate to make the right decisions because of fear—fear of judgment, failure, or losing favor. These fears whisper doubts:

- *"If I say what really needs to be said, will I be pushed out of the group?*
- *"If I confront this now, will I be seen as difficult or disloyal?*
- *"If I bring this forward, will this make me look like I'm not capable of my job?"*

These are the voices of self-preservation, deceiving your purpose; they aren't coming from your highest purpose-driven leadership. Transformative leaders learn to quiet these voices by anchoring themselves in what truly matters, choosing what serves the mission over what protects their position.

Often, when you dig deeper, you find the fears holding you back are less about real risks and more about imagined scenarios driven by ego.

When your actions match your values, you no longer carry the burden of constant doubt. The need to perform, manage perception, or second-guess your decisions disappears. There is a deep sense of calm and confidence that comes from knowing your leadership is rooted in truth, purpose, and acting in congruence with what you say you stand for.

The next chapter turns to the rare 10%—the leaders who chose differently. The ones who sacrificed their comfort to protect something far greater. And because of that, they didn't just lead through change. They became the reason change happened.

4

THE RARE 10%:
THE IDEAL ARCHETYPE

We now know that leaders don't fail because they lack purpose. They fail because they abandon it when it's tested. But a rare few—just 10%—did something different.

They faced risk. They sat at the same tables. They held the same power. They faced the same resistance, the same criticism, the same fear of what might be lost. But when pressure came, they didn't protect themselves—they protected the mission.

These weren't the loudest voices. They were the ones willing to stay in the tension, listen longer, ask better questions, and walk toward hard truths without demanding comfort first.

This chapter is not about perfection. It's about congruence with who you are. *Transformative* leadership doesn't begin when things are easy. It begins the moment you stop avoiding the tension and start leading through it.

This is the shift that separates the 10% of leaders from the 90%. And the difference begins with what you're about to see next: the 10%'s relationship with the truth.

The real test of leadership is how you respond to the truth—especially when it costs you something.

ARCHETYPE 4: PURPOSE-DRIVEN LEADERS WHO ARE TRANSFORMATIVE

High in Principles, High in Purpose
Key phrase: *Transparency of truth*
Outcome: *Ripple effect of positive impact*

Purpose-driven leaders who are transformative have found the sweet spot where their sense of purpose is unmistakable, and their principles are nonnegotiable. They embody their purpose in every action and decision. Their leadership isn't driven by trends or external pressures but by a deep, unshakable internal compass. They lead from their core, staying true to their mission even when faced with adversity.

Unlike performative leaders, they don't just talk about change—they create it. Unlike judgmental leaders, they don't enforce standards with criticism—they inspire people to rise. Unlike oppressive leaders, they don't avoid conflict to maintain harmony—they confront truth with clarity and courage.

WHAT CHARACTERIZES A TRANSFORMATIVE LEADER?

These leaders are distinguished by their unwavering commitment to a cause greater than themselves, prioritizing service to the greater good over personal gain. They consistently operate from a mindset of "we," focusing on collective success and shared purpose, rather than "me," which centers on individual preservation.

PURSUIT OF TRUTH

The defining difference between transformative leaders and everyone else is their relationship with the truth.

The 90% of leaders run from it. They avoid it. Minimize it. Dispute it. They fear how it will threaten their image, their control, or their comfort. They focus on what's unfavorable and dismiss what's inconvenient. Truth becomes something they are managing, not something to learn from.

But the 10%? They run straight into it. They don't treat truth as a personal attack; they treat it as essential intelligence.

Transformative leaders don't waste time defending their ego or preserving their image. They aren't caught up in who said it, how it was said, or whether it casts them in a favorable light. They pursue truth with the understanding that it rarely comes in absolutes.

They know all truth is shaped by context—relationships, history, emotion, and complexity. That's why they don't dismiss discomfort or critique. They treat truth as a data point: something to explore, weigh, and integrate. They ask: *What is this revealing? What are the implications?* This is what sets them apart. They let truth shape their decisions. As a result, innovation evolves, inclusion deepens, and performance excels.

I worked with a leader like this. A team member questioned a policy he had championed. He could've silenced the conversation to protect his pride. But he didn't. He listened. He examined what was said. He made the change. The policy improved, trust deepened, and his leadership elevated—not because he was right, but because he was open.

That's the difference.

The 90% suppress the truth to preserve their image or their comfort. The 10% seek the truth to expose blind spots and risks, in order to fuel their purpose, progress, and excellence.

Transparency is the biggest threat to those in power yet it's the single greatest determinant of transformative leadership.

TRANSPARENCY OF TRUTH

Truth alone is not enough. Truth only becomes powerful when it's brought forward, named, acknowledged, and revealed. Transparency is more than sharing information; it's about creating visibility into what's real, even when it's uncomfortable or unfavorable. Transformative leaders use transparency as the bridge between truth and trust, between what is known and what must be done.

Those who conceal reality may momentarily protect themselves, but in doing so, they weaken trust and allow dysfunction to take root.

I can tell you with certainty that transparency will absolutely create tension in the room. And that tension is exactly what most people fear because it threatens harmony, surfaces conflict, and challenges the unspoken rules of staying safe. However, it only becomes dangerous when leaders avoid the tension that truth creates.

When facilitated with proficiency, transparency invites dialogue that wouldn't otherwise happen. It surfaces disagreement, diverse perspectives, and difficult truths that are often avoided. And that's the point. Transparency stretches a team beyond silence and surface-level agreement; it pushes them toward clarity, alignment, and progress. And over time, it replaces fear with trust, and silence with shared responsibility.

One of my former colleagues exemplified transparency during a company restructuring. Faced with difficult workforce reductions, she chose clarity over silence, addressing the situation directly rather than allowing rumors and speculation to spread. In a company-wide meeting, she chose to share the financial challenges driving the changes. She explained the decision-making process, ensuring employees understood why choices were made, and acknowledged the impact of these decisions on individuals and teams. She also outlined the support being provided, including severance packages and career transition assistance.

Her willingness to reveal the rationale behind tough decisions, rather than shielding employees from harsh realities, built trust and credibility. It ensured that even in uncertainty, people felt valued and informed.

When people no longer ask, *"Will this be kept confidential?"* is when you know you have transformative leadership.

PRINCIPLES SERVING PURPOSE

"What's the right decision to make?"

It's a question every well-intended, purpose-driven leader believes they're answering correctly. They genuinely think they're doing what's best for the business. But that's where it gets complicated because the answer to that question depends entirely on *how* it's being measured.

The performative, judgmental, and even oppressive leader doesn't lack integrity. In fact, that's what makes them harder to spot. These leaders often see themselves as operating from high values. But without testing that against discomfort, ego, or self-interest, they miss their blind spot.

So here's the real test:

- Does this decision serve me or does it serve the greater mission?
- Does it protect a person or uphold a policy?
- Does it make me more comfortable or less?

These are the questions that reveal whether a leader is preserving self or leading with purpose.

This is where principles come in. When leaders are clear on the principles they will not betray in service of their purpose—no matter the risk to their image, identity, or favor—*that's* when you become unshakable.

Examples?

- **Transparency over protection**: Will you name the real issue, even when it implicates someone close to you?
- **Equity over preference**: Will you promote the person who challenges you, not just the one who's easiest to work with?
- **Truth over harmony**: Will you speak what needs to be said, even when it disrupts the room?

The right decision doesn't always feel good in the moment. But when it's guided by principle, it holds. That's the difference between a leader who wants change—and one who actually leads it.

Take the real-life story of Johnny Georges from *Shark Tank*. Johnny created the Tree T-Pee, an innovative water conservation product for farmers, and pitched it to the Sharks. During his presentation, he was challenged to justify his pricing model, which left little profit margin for him personally. The Sharks urged him to raise his prices to maximize earnings, essentially requiring it in order to get investors. But Johnny didn't budge. He explained that keeping the Tree T-Pee affordable was vital because it was designed to help struggling farmers, many of whom couldn't afford more expensive solutions.

As Johnny passionately explained, *"I'm not here to make millions; I'm here to make a difference."* His decision had Sharks say, *"I'm out."* But one Shark respected his principles and that Shark ultimately offered him a deal.

Johnny exemplifies what it means to lead with principles in service of purpose—aligning every decision with his mission. His unwavering stance nearly cost him the deal. He was willing to walk away rather than compromise. But ultimately, that same conviction is what earned him the investment. It's a powerful example of principle in action showing how staying true to purpose became the very reason for success.

Every leader will at some point face a moment when external pressure, internal fears, or the complexities of decision-making pull them away from their purpose.

I've worked with leaders who, under intense pressure, made decisions that didn't reflect their values. What set them apart was their willingness to own those missteps. They didn't double down, justify, or deflect. Instead, they protected the mission with actions like these:

- Acknowledged where they went wrong
- Reflected on what led to the misalignment
- Took action to correct it
- Communicated their course correction with transparency

They used their missteps as a moment of leadership. Realignment requires humility to admit when you've fallen short, courage to take personal ownership, and a willingness to grow from experience.

This is how you become part of the 10%.

REALIGNMENT IN ACTION

A Chief People Officer once resisted acknowledging the flaws in her organization's promotion process—not because she didn't care, but because she was afraid.

When concerns about favoritism were raised, her first reaction was to dismiss the feedback and defend the system, convinced it was fair. But when we reviewed the data together, a clear and undeniable pattern was shown: high-performing employees from certain demographic groups were being overlooked for leadership roles.

She became defensive and adamantly rejected the findings, insisting the data was wrong. Within a week, she ended our engagement altogether, citing a full plate and shifting priorities. She didn't speak to me for five months.

Then something shifted. She reached back out. She had been sitting with what was uncovered, unable to shake the weight of it. We met and she explained that she feared exposing the company to lawsuits. She feared being labeled or worse, that she would be seen as biased, especially toward employees from certain backgrounds that she saw herself as an advocate for.

That was the turning point for her. Her decision to reengage instead of avoid marked the beginning of her realignment.

She confronted the discomfort head-on and admitted that her defensiveness came from fear—not from facts. And that changed everything.

From there, we got to work. We didn't just tweak a few criteria—we rebuilt the entire process.

This required engaging in uncomfortable but critical conversations with the executive team, her own team, and other key stakeholders. We highlighted the relationship-based decisions that were embedded in the system. It wasn't easy. There was resistance from stakeholders, yet she remained committed and steadfast.

We revised the promotion standards to ensure consistency and objectivity. We facilitated talent reviews that calibrated evaluations across the same competencies, ensuring that identical behaviors were not being judged differently based on who exhibited them. We named the inconsistencies, course corrected in real time, and brought her entire leadership team into the process.

The executives and stakeholders weren't just told about the new process—they participated in it. They saw how fair it was. They experienced how structured, transparent, and rooted in **efficacy** it had become. What started as fear turned into transformation.

The result? A renewed culture of trust, credibility in succession planning, and a leader who realigned to her purpose—not by avoiding the hard truths, but by leading through them. Grievances declined. Lawsuits were avoided. And for the first time, employees believed the process was not only fair, but worth trusting.

THE LASTING IMPACT OF TRANSFORMATIVE LEADERSHIP

Transformative leaders set a new standard for how leadership should be done. Their influence doesn't stop at the organizational level; it reshapes the culture, communities, and even industries.

I've witnessed these leaders change not only how their companies operate, but how they show up in their families, friends, and everyday lives. They don't compartmentalize their leadership; they live it. The efficacy of their choices are consistent, whether they're leading a boardroom discussion or a conversation at the dinner table.

Efficacy is an underused word in leadership. Integrity gets most of the attention, and rightfully so, because values matter. But I use the word *efficacy* far more. Why? Because efficacy is about making decisions with the outcome and impact in mind. It's the long game that is focused on legacy and simultaneously sharpens the short game. When you're clear on the vision, you make more accurate short-term choices.

Integrity tells me what a leader values. Efficacy tells me whether those values actually work in real conditions, with real people, and real resistance.

This leadership is a way of life. It creates a ripple effect, redefining what people believe is possible when values aren't just spoken, but practiced. The most profound mark of a transformative leader isn't just what they achieve, but how they elevate those around them.

5

THE 5X5 FRAMEWORK: UNCOMPROMISED DECISION-MAKING

The 5x5 Framework is the *how* behind the Transformation Formula. It was born from a single question: How do 90% of leaders falter under the weight of ego—while only 10% drive true transformation?

It emerged from patterns observed behind closed doors—in rooms where those with the most power made decisions that shaped the conditions for everyone else yet faced no real consequences for those decisions. These were moments where truth had been named—about harm, exclusion, or leadership misalignment—and yet the only pressure present was internal: whether the leader would use their power to protect themselves or serve the greater cause.

In the environments where real breakthroughs occurred, a distinct set of behaviors repeatedly surfaced in the 10% of leaders who remained aligned with their purpose—even in the hardest moments:

1. **Vulnerability**
2. **Humility**
3. **Curiosity**
4. **Confronting**
5. **Transparency**

These five behaviors, which make up the right side of the 5x5, consistently unlocked trust, accelerated innovation, and sustained forward momentum—far beyond what leadership strategy or messaging alone could do.

COMPROMISED DECISIONS	UNCOMPROMISED DECISIONS
DEFENSIVE — A threat to identity or safety.	VULNERABILITY — An openness to the unknown.
ARROGANCE — A superiority mindset.	HUMILITY — A receptivity to learn.
IMPATIENCE — A quick fix.	CURIOSITY — A dive into complexity.
AVOIDANCE — A deflection of truth.	CONFRONTING — A capacity for tension.
CONTROL — Concealment to self protect.	TRANSPARENCY — Willingness to reveal.

It will be tempting to glance at the five behaviors on the right side of the 5x5 Framework and assume you already embody them. So did the 90%. It is not uncommon for leaders to recognize these five words, only to dismiss them as things they have already achieved. Meanwhile, their team members confide in me, expressing concern and uncertainty about when meaningful change will occur. They ask, *"Will this be kept confidential?"* and then share all the ways this leader does not embody the right side of the 5x5.

This is where the intersection of power, self-preservation, and purpose becomes pivotal. When power is held without consequences, self-protection becomes a seductive default. Leaders convince themselves they're acting in service of the greater good. But power without principle erodes purpose.

Through my work, I also found that when purpose-driven leaders consistently operated from the left side of the 5x5, their leadership displayed these behaviors:

1. **Defensiveness**
2. **Arrogance**
3. **Impatience**
4. **Avoidance**
5. **Control**

Operating from the left side of the 5x5; they trade purpose for self-preservation. They use their position to shield themselves from being challenged rather than to advance what's right. The most dangerous part? These decisions are rarely visible to others—but they define everything that follows.

These behaviors weren't deliberate acts of harm. Instead, they showed up as reflexes—automatic responses designed to protect identity, authority, or status. Each time a leader responded this way, their decisions drifted further from their intended purpose and led to outcomes that directly contradicted the very change they were trying to create.

This is how ineffective leadership takes hold. Not through lack of intent but through repeated compromise. Leaders don't set out to be performative, judgmental, or oppressive. But when ego, fear, or self-preservation take the lead, these become the default behaviors behind decisions and the way their power is misused. This discovery is what reshaped my definition of *integrity*, as *the ability to distinguish* when interactions or choices are compromised or uncompromised. This definition of integrity offers a new standard by which I guide and support leaders to lead with unwavering alignment to their values even in the hardest moments.

This is what makes the 5x5 Framework so critical—and so transformational. It can predict the likely trajectory of a relationship, or the effectiveness of a decision, by identifying the origination point through the lens of the 5x5.

The 5x5 reveals that only when leaders make uncompromised decisions can they truly claim to lead with integrity. The implications of this discovery are profound: it challenges traditional notions of integrity and replaces them with a measurable, actionable standard for leadership.

WHEN TO USE THE 5X5 FRAMEWORK

The 5x5 should be activated in real time, especially in moments where power, truth, and pressure intersect. Use it when . . .

- You are sharing hard truths
- You are giving or receiving feedback
- You are navigating conflict or tension
- You are hearing or presenting data, reports, or insights
- You are listening to information that challenges your perspective
- You are about to make a decision
- You are being asked to influence or to be influenced

Whether you hold power or are trying to influence it, the model applies equally. It offers behavioral precision in complex situations, helping you close the gap between what you intend and what others experience.

When interactions and decisions are shaped by these behaviors, the health of relationships is preserved and decisions stay uncorrupted, giving them the highest chance of success.

WHAT IS AN UNCOMPROMISED VS. A COMPROMISED DECISION?

DEFINING AN UNCOMPROMISED INTERACTION OR DECISION

A decision or interaction is uncompromised when the right side of the 5x5 is being displayed—when the behaviors of vulnerability, humility, curiosity, confronting, and transparency are present.

This means the starting place of that choice is pure, and the destiny of that moment has the highest potential of success. The outcome—however it develops—is shaped by honesty without any distortion. So what unfolds from that moment ripples outward with momentum toward the highest good.

That's what makes this so powerful: you can predict the success of an outcome by the purity of the seed it starts from. When a decision begins with the right side of the 5x5 and continues to be nurtured by those same behaviors, then like any living system, what you plant—and how you care for it—shapes what it becomes. When the seed is pure, and the nourishment consistent, the outcome grows in the direction of healthy transformation. It unfolds with integrity because it started that way.

The real difference between the 90% of leaders who falter and the 10% who remain transformative isn't their desire to lead change. It's whether their behaviors align with the outcome they claim to want.

DEFINING A COMPROMISED INTERACTION OR DECISION

A decision or interaction is compromised when the left side of the 5x5 is in play—when defensiveness, arrogance, impatience, avoidance, or control are driving the moment.

This means the starting place of that choice is already corrupted, so the destiny of that moment has no potential to serve the highest good. The result—whatever it becomes—is shaped by distortion. And what unfolds from that moment ripples outward in a pattern of breakdown—missteps, mistrust, and harm.

That's what makes this so imperative: you can predict the failure of an outcome by the seed it starts with. When a decision begins on the left side of the 5x5, the seed being planted is already a weed.

From that very first moment, its growth is set. It doesn't just delay success—it grows unhealthy dynamics and dysfunction. It spreads quickly, chokes out progress, and multiplies distortion.

When the seed is compromised from the start and the same behaviors continue, the outcome is already on a path toward erosion. It cannot produce transformation until the pattern is interrupted by the right side of the 5x5.

Leaders who default to ego-driven reactions don't just stall progress—they unintentionally reinforce the very issues they're trying to dismantle.

Let's look at how each of the ego-driven behaviors infiltrates leadership, is the beginning source for the status quo, and causes the most repeated statement I hear inside companies attempting culture change: "*They will never change.*"

DEFENSIVENESS: THE REFLEX TO PROTECT, NOT PROCESS

A THREAT TO IDENTITY OR SAFETY

Defensiveness is a subconscious response to something we don't want to feel within ourselves. Leaders don't become defensive simply because feedback is difficult; they become defensive when feedback touches on an unresolved fear or perceived weakness.

Defensiveness in purpose-driven leaders generally arises when there's a disconnect between their self-perception and how their leadership—and their power—is being experienced by others. It feels less like feedback and more like a personal threat to their identity or authority. It arises almost instinctively and often immediately when a leader feels their sincerity, credibility, or core identity is being attacked. It's a gut-level reaction that triggers an urge to counter, reject, or rationalize something unfavorable that has been brought to their attention.

Within the framework, defensiveness typically surfaces in situations of public exposure such as meetings, workshops, or coaching discussions.

Defensiveness in action:

- **Reactive rebuttal**: Quickly countering or shifting blame that reflects ownership. *"That's not from my team; it came from your team."*
- **Projecting**: Accusing the other person of behaviors the individual is displaying themselves. *"They're being critical and disrespectful, not me."*
- **Rejecting**: Shutting down or refusing to engage because it causes discomfort or threatens identity. *"I don't have time for this kind of negativity—I'm moving on."*

Defensiveness rejects unpleasant information but also justifies continuing unchanged behaviors. It allows leaders to continue operating as they always have, all while believing they are still acting in good faith.

EXAMPLE

There is a notable instance from October 2024 where Dallas Cowboys owner Jerry Jones was defensive during a media interaction. In a radio interview on 105.3 The Fan, following a significant 47–9 loss to the Detroit Lions, Jones was questioned about the team's offseason decisions and their potential impact on the team's performance. He reacted sharply, stating:

"Now if you think I'm interested in a damn phone call with you over the radio and sitting here and throwing all the good out with the dishwater, you'd have got to be smoking something over there this morning. I'm not. And I really don't . . . and I don't even want our listeners listening to me talk about.

"This is not your job. Your job isn't to let me go over the reasons that I did something and I'm sorry that I did it. That's not your job. That's not your job, or I'll get somebody else to ask these questions, men. No, no. I'm not kidding. You're not going to figure out what the team is doing right or wrong. . . Y'all really think you're going to sit here with a microphone and tell me all of the things that I've done wrong and without going over the rights?"

Jerry has faced heavy criticism since taking over the Cowboys, which may earn him some room for defensiveness. But the Cowboys haven't reached a Super Bowl since their 1995 victory. Defensiveness isn't the answer. Face the tough truths and unlock the ideas that can bring championships back.

This self-protective reflex lets the leader persist in their current attitude or actions. It enables them to reject constructive evaluation or responsibility.

The result? Defensiveness turns into an invisible permission slip that sanctions dysfunction, excuses harm, or keeps progress at a standstill.

ARROGANCE: WHEN AUTHORITY ENABLES DISMISSIVENESS

A SUPERIORITY MINDSET

It's rare for purpose-driven leaders to be associated with arrogance especially because of the ideals they express about why they lead. Their values often center around change, service, and inclusion. But that's precisely what makes this form of arrogance so hard to detect.

When **power + ego + purpose** intersect, it can produce a quiet sense of superiority—masked as sincerity. It shows up not through overt dominance, but through subtle forms of dismissiveness: *a quiet defiance that relegates something significant as insignificant.*

Arrogance is one of the most prevalent yet least discussed behaviors in leadership, especially at the highest levels of power where oversight is minimal and accountability is diluted. But it isn't exclusive to senior leaders. In fact, some of the most passionate, purpose-driven individuals committed to making a difference can unknowingly exhibit arrogance, not out of malice, but out of cynicism or contempt.

While arrogance often brings to mind egotism or self-importance, in this context, it shows up as an overestimation of one's competence in areas where subject matter expertise is lacking, yet authority is still exercised. It's the confidence to lead change without the humility to learn first.

I've seen this in well-intentioned leaders at all levels, many of whom have experienced marginalization themselves. Because they see themselves as advocates or experts, they may resist input, side-step collaboration, or assert their way of doing things as the right way. Their belief in the mission overrides their willingness to build bridges, gain proficiency, or grow from others' leadership. In short, their commitment to the cause becomes the very reason they stop learning how to lead it.

Arrogance uses intellect, authority, or experience to dominate, silence, or suppress rather than elevate or include. There's an unconscious pride that one's insight is simply more valid.

Arrogance in action:

- **Weaponizing**: Using knowledge, influence, or experience to control conversations or assert dominance in the situation. *"This feels like a psychological safety violation—I don't feel safe being questioned like this."* (Weaponizes the language of safety to deflect discomfort when being held accountable.)

- **Dismissiveness**: Minimizing or disregarding others' perspectives or value, often through nonverbal cues or condescending responses. *"This information doesn't apply here—let's move on."* (Dismisses insights to reinforce own authority and resist outside influence.)

- **Superiority**: Operating with an internal belief that one's contributions, ideas, or position are more valid, important, or correct than others'. *"They haven't been here long enough to have a real say—they need to earn their place first."* (Uses tenure as a superiority metric to undermine new voices or perspectives.)

EXAMPLE

An executive was promoted to lead an enterprise-wide innovation initiative. She had a proven track record in operations and execution, but limited experience in innovation strategy, design thinking, or user-centered development. Despite this, she took charge with absolute confidence and dismissed the expertise of others.

When members of the innovation team proposed a phased approach involving cross-functional input, customer discovery, and prototyping, she shut it down:

"We don't need all that. We already know what our customers want."

Throughout the initiative, she relied on instinct and her past success rather than evidence or collaborative input. She overrode team concerns, rejected iterative processes, and viewed dissent as being disrespectful to her authority.

Because she believed her leadership strength in other domains automatically translated to innovation, she unintentionally stifled the very thing she believed wholeheartedly in. Instead of fostering experimentation and risk-taking, she expected compliance. As a result, the best ideas never made it off the whiteboard, and the organization missed an opportunity to evolve.

Dismissiveness, fueled by a sense of superiority and reinforced by positional authority, is the most common way arrogance shows up—and the most overlooked. Without addressing arrogance, leaders perpetuate a cycle of surface-level efforts that never truly challenges the status quo.

IMPATIENCE: THE CYCLE OF STARTING AND STOPPING

A QUICK, EASY FIX

For leaders driven by change, action feels urgent—and necessary. The mindset is clear: *We don't need to talk about it; we need to do something about it.* In many cases, this bias toward action is an asset. But for leaders who are quick to act, impatience becomes a hidden threat to meaningful change. Impatience reflects a belief that *A + B = C*, assuming a single or linear activity will immediately yield the desired outcome.

What caused 90% of purpose-driven leaders to unintentionally prevent change—even while taking action—was this: impatience was directly tied to the cognitive strain to process nuance and work through complexity. As a result, they oversimplified issues because they lacked the tolerance for doing the deeper, more demanding work required to address the issues accurately.

The preference for simplicity drives leaders to rush through processes, cut corners, or skip essential steps to achieve what they perceive as "fast progress." It might involve pressuring teams to meet unrealistic deadlines, dismissing the need for further examination, or abandoning long-term strategies in favor of short-term wins. Recognizing this underlying cognitive discomfort is essential because it shifts the focus from simply managing timelines to addressing the leader's capacity to embrace and process complexity.

Impatience in action:

- **Acting**: Moving ahead without alignment or input to relieve urgency rather than achieve readiness. *"We don't have time to wait* *for everyone to catch up—progress requires momentum."* (Justifies bypassing alignment by framing urgency as leadership.)

- **Deciding**: Making hasty or uninformed choices that bypass deeper understanding, feedback, or collaboration. *"It's better to make a quick decision than get stuck in analysis paralysis."* (Frames speed as decisiveness.)

- **Instructing**: Giving direction to expedite progress rather than build ownership or clarity. *"I know what needs to be done—explaining it will only slow things down."* (Uses efficiency as a rationale for skipping key, necessary steps.)

Impatience is a push toward speed over substance. It sacrifices accuracy for false efficiency.

EXAMPLE

I worked with an organization where employees voiced growing frustration because the company's public values didn't
reflect their lived experience. Despite being nationally recognized as a "Best Employer," the internal culture told a very
different story. Skepticism had settled in: "*We've done this ten
times. Nothing changes.*"

Employees had seen too many initiatives launched and
abandoned—each one claiming to take culture seriously, only
to fade when real change demanded more than a training, a
new slogan, or a rebranded set of values.

This time, the organization was given a strategic, phased
plan designed to achieve the transformation they said they
wanted. It included detailed recommendations for revising
outdated policies and rebuilding core systems—recruitment,
promotions, and performance evaluations—to reflect their
values in practice. It was a roadmap for sustainable change.

But the leadership team were frustrated by it and ignored
it. Instead, they defaulted to surface-level actions: rewriting the
company values, launching a values committee, and scheduling employee trainings. They believed those activities would fix
the problem—quick, visible efforts that didn't require deeper
work on their own behaviors or systemic blind spots.

And just as the employees predicted, the initiative discon-
tinued prematurely.

The executive leaders on the team who lacked political
favor with the CEO *did* see the potential of the strategy but
remained silent. Two executives opted to step down from the
leadership team and two others left the organization altogether.

This story is an all too familiar example of how impatience kills transformation. Executives demand quick results without understanding the complexity of the issue. Employees see through the superficial efforts and disengage further. Rather than committing to real change, they abandon the effort and move on to the next initiative. The cycle repeats, leaving employees more disillusioned and skeptical each time.

AVOIDANCE: CONVENIENCE OVER SUBSTANCE

A DEFLECTION OF TENSION

This dynamic plagues executive leadership teams the most. Despite holding the highest authority, many still avoid addressing real issues—not because they don't see them, but because the environment at the top is often fractured by power dynamics, unspoken divisions, and silent imbalance of favor. Even at this level, psychological safety is fragile. Those who hold political currency dominate the space, while others operate in quiet self-protection, choosing survival over truth.

Avoidance, in this context, is one of the most subtle yet most pervasive forms of deflection. Among the 90% of leaders who abandoned their values and commitment to creating change, avoidance was driven by discomfort with the emotional complexity of situations, especially when those situations required introspection or examining their own leadership.

While these leaders could address external issues with ease, the moment the focus turned inward, avoidance manifested as a self-protective behavior. They would not risk the tension that could strain relationships, challenge their image, or jeopardize their status.

Avoidance doesn't always look like outright denial. Instead, it appears as a masterful dance around the topic: deflecting, rationalizing, or redirecting the conversation in ways that allow the leader to avoid confronting the truth, whether consciously or subconsciously. For example, a leader might redirect a discussion about their own role in a team's dysfunction to broader organizational challenges, presenting their deflection as insightful commentary while sidestepping personal ownership.

Because this behavior is often exhibited so sophisticatedly, recognizing deflection requires a high level of awareness. It is most common among leaders who are accustomed to being high performers or highly trusted, which creates a psychological barrier to acknowledging their own contributions to an issue. The more a leader's identity is tied to their track record of acceptance, likeability, or success, the harder it becomes to accept responsibility when something isn't working.

What holds leaders back from confrontation isn't usually logic. It's the emotional toll it takes. They avoid difficult conversations because . . .

- They assume the issue is small, not realizing its compounding impact.
- They fear damaging relationships when in reality, avoidance erodes trust faster.
- They are uncomfortable with tension, failing to see that tension already exists beneath the surface.
- They believe moving past an issue is the same as resolving it—but it's not.

Avoidance in action:

- **Deflecting**: Shifting attention away from difficult topics or personal responsibility through humor, redirection, or silence. *"Let's not get stuck on that—we can circle back later."*
- **Minimizing**: Discounting the importance of issues, feelings, or experiences—whether your own or others'. *"I don't think it's that big of a deal."*

- **Distancing**: Invalidating another's reality or emotional experience as exaggerated, unimportant, or inconvenient. *"The data isn't relevant for this, we just need a morale boost."*

EXAMPLE

During a strategy meeting, an executive leadership team I worked with set out to address declining employee engagement and rising turnover. An HR team member had gathered both qualitative and quantitative data, uncovering deep-seated cultural issues. The findings revealed patterns of disengagement, perceived favoritism, and leadership behaviors that left employees feeling underutilized and unheard.

Uncomfortable with the depth of these issues, the HR executive blocked the data and discussion and instead helped spearhead an initiative to introduce company awards, believing it would provide a quick morale boost. Employees were asked to vote on categories like "All-Around Leader," "Unsung Hero," and "Service to Others," and the final winners were ultimately hand-selected by the executive team.

Rather than improving engagement, the awards fueled resentment and further alienated employees. The same well-connected individuals won, leaving even those closest to them feeling frustrated and overlooked. Whispers spread: *"I don't want to attend the awards ceremony because it's all for show."* and *"She says she wants change, but she keeps benefiting from her relationships with leadership and playing along."*

Instead of addressing the root causes of disengagement, the initiative amplified distrust in leadership and reinforced to employees that their real concerns weren't being acknowledged, let alone addressed.

Deflection stunts personal growth, reinforces blind spots, and erodes trust with teams. Employees perceive avoidance as a lack of courage or competence, leading to disengagement and diminished respect for leadership.

Unaddressed issues don't disappear—they compound. Avoidance delays decisions, deepens dysfunction, and erodes engagement. The longer leaders sidestep discomfort, the harder it becomes to move forward—and the higher the cost to progress.

CONTROL: THE ULTIMATE BARRIER TO CHANGE

CONCEALING OR SUPPRESSING THE TRUTH

Of all the ego-driven behaviors, control is the most dangerous—because it is the most disguised. Purpose-driven leaders rarely see themselves as concealing or suppressing through control. Many leaders conceal because they believe they are protecting the company, others, or themselves. They tell themselves it is caution, not control. But over time, these protective instincts became patterns of suppression: shielding uncomfortable truths, avoiding accountability, and managing perceptions that perpetuated further harm. This is where power is most misused: not through overt domination, but through subtle decisions to reshape the truth.

Control was the common denominator that showed up alongside defensiveness, arrogance, impatience, and avoidance—because these purpose-driven leaders also held power. Unlike other ego-driven behaviors, control is rarely seen in isolation. It doesn't just coexist—it amplifies the impact of every other behavior around it.

Examples:

- **Defensiveness through control** – Rejects feedback and uses positional power to discontinue coaching: *"I don't need coaching,"* using authority to outweigh personal ownership.
- **Arrogance through control** – Dismisses expertise and uses positional power to override advisement: *"We're going in this direction,"* which increases legal vulnerabilities.
- **Impatience through control** – Issues directives and uses positional power to convey expectation: *"Just follow my directions."*
- **Avoidance through control** – Is uncomfortable with information and uses positional power to suppress it: *"We're not discussing this,"* thereby minimizing unfavorable data.

This pattern reveals a critical equation:

Power + Ego = Status Quo

Control is the ultimate barrier to transformation because it prevents truth from surfacing, blocks ownership, and protects the status quo. The more power a leader holds, the easier it becomes to shield their image or avoid discomfort without realizing it. What feels like protection is actually preservation of self, at the cost of progress.

At its core, control is the exertion of power to maintain certainty, influence, or emotional safety. It limits collaboration, transparency, and psychological safety, the very conditions required for a healthy organizational culture.

Control in action:

- **Concealing**: Withholding information to maintain power or manage perception. *"Sharing too much just* *opens the door for criticism—we need to stay in control of the message."*

- **Suppressing**: Silencing emotional expression, dissent, or differing views to avoid disruption or maintain a sense of order. *"Let's not open that up right now—it'll only stir up negativity and distract us from the real work."*
- **Overriding**: Dismissing input, autonomy, or collaborative process to force a decision or outcome. *"I'm not debating this—I've already made the call."*

EXAMPLE

A department leader was tasked with selecting team members for a high-visibility project that came with executive exposure and the potential for promotion. Rather than establishing clear criteria or opening the opportunity to applicants, she quietly handpicked a few individuals behind the scenes.

When other team members learned of the project through internal chatter—after it had already launched—they asked why they hadn't been considered. The leader responded vaguely: *"It was a fast-moving decision, and I had to go with who I knew could handle it."*

In reality, she feared that opening the process would lead to pushback and hard conversations. To maintain control, she kept the selection process concealed.

But the fallout was immediate. Team members began questioning her fairness and integrity. Some assumed decisions were based on favoritism or political alliances. Others stopped raising their hands for opportunities, believing the system was rigged.

Her intent was to keep things "simple and smooth." The result was the opposite: fractured trust, lowered morale, and widening perceptions of inequity. By believing she could control the narrative she unintentionally created the very dysfunction she was trying to avoid.

No real change—personal, cultural, or organizational—can occur as long as power is being used to suppress what needs to be addressed. Control may feel like protection, but it often functions as obstruction. Leaders will often convince themselves they're safeguarding the company—especially from legal or reputational risk—when in reality, they're creating greater exposure by concealing truth and suppressing dissent.

This is where truth becomes the greatest prevention of change—not because it's harmful, but because it gets stifled.

When truth is withheld to maintain control, progress halts.

CONSEQUENCES OF SELF-PRESERVATION AND SELF-PROTECTION

Each of the archetypes—performative, judgmental, and oppressive—stood at the same crossroad: the moment when truth surfaced and the stakes felt personal. In each case, something uncomfortable or unfavorable was exposed about the business, about themselves, or about their colleagues. And in that defining moment, they abandoned the mission because they abandoned their courage. Instead of choosing purpose, they chose self-protection, reacting with defensiveness, arrogance, impatience, avoidance or control.

These weren't passive responses. They were choices. Here's the most unsettling truth: these purpose-driven leaders knew. They were not unaware of the dysfunction, favoritism, oppression, or harm occurring around them. They knew when poor behavior was being permitted, when exclusion and sabotage were happening and to whom, when credit was stolen or when someone was being unfairly discredited. They knew when certain processes were insufficient and they knew the impact it was having—not just on individuals, but on the very mission they wanted to champion. And still, they did nothing.

Why? Because taking action was seen as being an admission of oversight, of complicity, or of failure to lead. And in their minds, admission felt too close to personal risk. It wasn't actual risk. Their power wasn't truly in jeopardy. Their positions were secure. Their influence was intact. The organization wouldn't have collapsed if they addressed the truth—on the contrary, it had the potential to accelerate performance, rebuild trust, and elevate the culture. But their egos couldn't see that.

Instead, they misjudged the threat. They believed that acknowledging the truth would tarnish their image, call their credibility into question, or destabilize their reputations. In reality, naming the truth would have made them stronger and their companies far healthier. It could have advanced the company. It could have become a defining moment of leadership. But their fear was grounded in personal consequence. It was rooted in perception. So they protected the status quo, and missed the opportunity to lead.

And that is the cost of self-preservation: what could have been a moment of transformation becomes a moment of erosion—not just of trust, but of purpose, performance, and progress.

In the short term, they succeeded.

They kept their position. They preserved their image. They kept their friendships intact. They kept things safe.

But here's what was actually lost:

- **The company's evolution stalled**. The culture didn't transform—it conformed. Innovation was stifled because safety became more important than risk.
- **Talent left—or stayed disengaged**. The very people who could have elevated the business quietly withdrew. Their brilliance, their ideas, their commitment were never fully accessed.
- **Momentum died in the silence**. Meetings continued, strategies were revised, KPIs updated—but the mission lost its heartbeat. The organization kept moving, but it wasn't progressing.
- **Purpose was held hostage by the ego**. Not just once, but repeatedly—until the mission became more of a slogan than a standard.

And at the personal level?

What was lost wasn't just professional credibility; it was something far more personal. A slow disconnection from the self. Most people will never know what happened in those closed-door conversations. The NDAs, the unspoken rules, the small circle of decision-makers—these protect the story. But you know. Your conscience knows. Your body carries it. Your heart remembers.

You still leave the office and go home. You sit across from loved ones. You lay your head on the pillow at night. And even if no one else will ever ask you about it—you will. In quiet moments, the cost resurfaces.

You didn't just bypass the truth. You bypassed who you intended to be. Your conviction gave way to convenience. Your courage got edged out by calculation. And while you may still hold the position and still be seen as successful, something essential was lost in the exchange. Greatness. Excellence. Exceptionalism. These are not guaranteed or granted by success. They are built by something deeper. Because success can be achieved through performance. But success and greatness are not the same.

Greatness is an insatiable dissatisfaction with the status quo—paired with the rare capacity to hold deep impatience for what must change while practicing extraordinary patience with who is changing. It is the pursuit of better—not for personal gain, but in service of your highest values for the highest good.

Greatness demands congruence—a full alignment between who you are, what you believe, and how you lead. It requires wholeness—the integration of worthiness and significance—and the strength to push beyond your own comfort in ways that elevate others. Greatness is reserved for those willing to refine power, use it with principle, and remain unwavering in purpose—even when it demands the sacrifice of self for the collective good.

Self-preservation may look like wisdom. It may feel like control. But it is a form of erosion of self. Quiet. Cumulative. And devastating.

These aren't minor decisions. These are pivotal moments. The kind that define the legacy you leave, not just in what you built, but in what you refused to face.

What follows in the next chapter is not theory—it's the path back. Even though self-preservation may have taken the lead, it is never too late to reclaim the purpose, principles, and power that define transformative leadership.

The 5x5 Framework helps you identify these patterns, shedding insight into how and why they emerge. By recognizing these behaviors as self-preservation, you can shift from reactive, ego-driven interactions and decisions to choices that align with your highest potential.

6

LEADING FROM THE RIGHT SIDE OF THE 5X5

Every decision a leader makes has an outcome based on its origin. Decisions made from ego, self-preservation, or fear lead to short-term fixes, fractured relationships, and repeated cycles of dysfunction. But decisions made in support of purpose create lasting impact, break historical barriers, and drive transformation that outlives the leaders themselves.

The 10% of purpose-driven leaders who upheld their commitments at the crossroads in pivotal moments understood this. They acknowledged the dynamics of their relationships, the culture within their teams, and the development of their organizations all originated from their decisions. And while others relied on authority, experience, or position to justify decisions, these leaders operated from a different barometer: five distinct characteristics that shaped the destiny of their decisions: vulnerability, humility, curiosity, confronting, and transparency.

These were the origination points of transformational change. Progress was no longer dictated by ego but by purpose. They built cultures where disagreement and debate thrived, where decisions weren't about optics or control, but focused on efficacy.

These five characteristics are the barometer for transformative leadership. They serve as a litmus test for whether interactions and decisions will sustain progress or reinforce stagnation. This chapter will break down each behavior not as a buzzword but as the essential conditions for influence, trust, and transformation. The leaders who master these behaviors aren't just making better choices; they are ensuring their behaviors and decisions have the power to reshape systems, teams, and organizations.

VULNERABILITY: THE STRENGTH TO STAND IN UNCERTAINTY

THE WILLINGNESS TO EMBRACE THE UNKNOWN

Vulnerability is the single most difficult place for leaders to be—especially when they're in a room together. In collective leadership spaces, where authority, image, and influence are silently negotiated, the idea of revealing uncertainty or owning mistakes can feel like risking power itself.

But within the 5x5 Framework, vulnerability is defined by a leader's willingness to engage with uncertainty—uncertainty about how their truth will be received, what it might expose about their competence or character, or how it may shift others' perceptions of them. Accepting the unknown means stepping forward without guarantees—without knowing if honesty will be met with respect or resistance, or if transparency will strengthen or weaken their influence.

Vulnerability requires choosing truth anyway. It's a deliberate release of control in service of authenticity and growth—something that runs counter to the protective instincts most leaders have spent years perfecting.

Vulnerability is most tested when difficult truths are spoken—especially when those truths reveal a disconnect between a leader's intent and their actual impact. It's one thing to own a visible mistake. It's another to sit with the discomfort of hearing that your actions, though well-meaning, have caused harm, confusion, or disengagement.

This is where vulnerability requires the most courage: not in admitting failure, but in receiving unflattering feedback without defensiveness. It means resisting the urge to explain, justify, or fix and instead choosing to listen, acknowledge, and absorb. When a leader can say, "That wasn't my intent, but I see how it impacted you," they demonstrate a rare strength: the ability to hold space for someone else's truth while still standing in their own.

Vulnerability in action:

- **Exposing**: Willingly revealing inner thoughts, mistakes, fears, or needs—not to seek validation, but to build trust. *"I've been second-guessing some of my decisions lately, and I want to be transparent about that with this group."*
- **Receptivity**: Remaining open and present to others' emotions, perspectives, or information—even when they challenge your own. *"I may not fully understand your experience yet, but I want to."*
- **Receiving**: Taking in feedback, impact, or truth without immediate defense or denial. *"I see how that landed, and I appreciate you telling me—even though it's hard to hear."*

EXAMPLE

In a team meeting, after receiving feedback about their leadership style making some employees feel dismissed, a director paused and said, *"I didn't realize I was doing that. I need to hear this—even if it's hard."* He didn't explain it away or shift blame. He listened, took notes, and followed up with one-on-ones later that week. That moment shifted how the team saw him. They saw him as willing, and as a result, he became more respected.

Vulnerability reflects emotional resilience and a commitment to growth. This is what made the 10% of leaders who embraced vulnerability so noteworthy.

HUMILITY: LEADING WITH HEALTHY SELF-DOUBT

THE POWER OF CO-OWNERSHIP

We often mislabel what is actually *healthy humility* as imposter syndrome. Not every moment of self-doubt is pathological—sometimes it's just truth. Especially when stepping into a role that feels bigger than our experience, humility becomes a necessary strength, not a flaw. It is the internal acknowledgment: *"I'm still growing into this."* For many leaders, particularly those newly tasked with managing people, departments, or entire companies, it's not imposter syndrome they're feeling; it's the weight of responsibility they now carry. And we need more of that.

True humility is not about insecurity. It's about being grounded in reality and self-awareness, recognizing that power doesn't equate to preparedness and that authority doesn't replace the need for collaboration. It allows leaders to rise into their roles while still honoring the gaps they must navigate with care, curiosity, and input from others.

Among the 10% of leaders who upheld their purpose during pivotal moments, humility was a defining trait. While others defaulted to self-reliance, especially under pressure, these leaders chose to co-own decisions with those closest to the issue. They sought subject matter expertise as a critical component of integrity-driven decision-making.

What made this so remarkable was its rarity. Most leaders feel the pressure to appear certain, to lead from a place of absolute authority. But the most transformative leaders had the courage to say, *"I don't know enough about this yet—help me understand."*

By seeking input and co-sharing decisions with those who had critical expertise, these leaders gave their decisions the chance to achieve a result grounded in efficacy and aligned with the intended purpose.

Humility in action:

- **Acknowledging**: Recognizing the limits of your knowledge, the strengths of others, and the role everyone plays in shared success. *"I may not have all the answers here—your experience in this area is deeper than mine, and I respect that."*

- **Inviting**: Actively seeking out perspectives, feedback, or dissent because you believe others have value to add. *"I'd really like to hear how you see this. What am I missing that you think we need to consider before we move forward?"*

- **Adjusting**: Being willing to shift your belief, behavior, or decision when new insights or truths emerge. *"You've raised a valid point I hadn't fully considered. I'm going to revisit this approach and make some changes."*

EXAMPLE

She had just stepped into the chief marketing officer role—charged with overseeing departments well outside her prior experience. The pressure to prove herself was palpable, but instead of defaulting to authority or pretending to have all the answers, she chose a different path.

She opened her first cross-functional department meeting by saying, *"I'll be honest—some of this is outside my depth. My job isn't to have all the answers, but to make sure we get to the best one. I'll be leaning on each of you to guide our decisions in your areas."*

That moment of humility set the tone. Because there had already been quiet resistance to her promotion, her admission didn't undermine her credibility—it dismantled the whispers. By openly acknowledging what others were already questioning, she diffused the tension and earned greater respect. Her humility disarmed the critics and disempowered the naysayers.

Her leadership wasn't weakened by that admission—it was strengthened. By creating space for others to lead in their areas of strength, she led more effectively in hers.

Humility prioritizes growth over pride.

CURIOSITY: THE DISCIPLINE TO DELAY

THE CAPACITY FOR COMPLEXITY

The quickest way to spot curiosity in a leader isn't through their ideas—it's through their questions. Curious leaders distinguish themselves by responding with questions rather than statements. They pause instead of push. They explore before they execute. And in doing so, they often surface truths that would otherwise go unnoticed.

Among the 10% of transformative leaders, this habit stood out. Where others rushed to direct or decide, these leaders resisted the urge to react. Instead, they asked a question first.

This wasn't because they had extra time; it was because they understood that slowing down was the only way to lead with accuracy. They didn't simplify complexity to move faster; they engaged with it to lead smarter.

Curiosity gave them the discipline to navigate discomfort, resist assumptions, and interrupt ingrained patterns that no longer served their teams or organizations. Instead of defaulting to fast but incomplete solutions, they made space for critical thinking and explored whether their actions would actually produce the intended outcome or simply check a box.

Curiosity in action:

- **Exploring**: Asking thoughtful questions to uncover context, root causes, or unseen perspectives—especially before acting, deciding, or responding. *"Is this the best way forward, or just the most familiar?"*
- **Listening**: Paying attention beyond words to tone, body language, and what's unsaid. It values what the other person

is truly trying to communicate. *"Am I reacting to urgency, or am I truly solving the root issue?"*

- **Pausing**: Intentionally creating space to reflect, absorb, and consider before jumping to solutions. *"Am I willing to challenge my own thinking, even if it means delaying action?"*

Curiosity isn't only about seeking knowledge; it is about having the discipline to resist urgency so decisions are accurate, whole, and complete.

In leadership, impatience often disguises itself as decisiveness. But truly transformative leaders understand that wisdom requires restraint, and that curiosity is the willingness to delay action in service of a better outcome.

EXAMPLE

A striking example of this tension unfolds in *House of the Dragon*, season 2, episode 8. Queen Rhaenyra Targaryen, under pressure from Prince Daemon, is expected to initiate war. Daemon is urgent, emotional, and ready to strike—a classic display of impatience masked as readiness. But Rhaenyra pauses. She knows that acting now—without fully securing her alliances—could destroy everything she's trying to protect.

And I'll admit—even I got impatient watching it. I was calling out at the screen, *"Come on, do something!"* I couldn't take the suspense. But that's the point. Impatience wants resolution, even when the timing is wrong. Rhaenyra's choice made *me* uncomfortable, because she was doing what most leaders avoid: sitting in the tension and asking, *What's still unknown? What alliances aren't solid yet? What could this cost us if we move too soon?*

Her refusal to rush wasn't weakness. It's strategy. It's intentionality. She asks, *"What do we not yet know? Who do we still need? What could we lose if we act now?"*

In contrast, Daemon's impatience pushes him to undermine her authority, unable to tolerate the space between deliberation and action.

Rhaenyra's decision ultimately earns her the support of key allies, including her aunt, Princess Rhaenys, and Lord Corlys Velaryon—who come to respect her *composure*. Her willingness to wait opened the door for deeper allegiance. Her curiosity, her willingness to explore before executing, becomes her power.

And while that may be fiction, the tension it reflects is very real. I've seen this same dynamic play out in boardrooms, strategy sessions, and executive offsites.

Curiosity doesn't mean indecision. It means refusing to be pulled by urgency when the stakes demand wisdom.

Curiosity is what drove the 10% of transformative leaders to take a different course of action. It allowed them to reverse processes and practices rooted in convenience and instead create intentional, thoughtful approaches.

Curiosity signals respect for complexity and a desire to get it right, not just fast.

CONFRONTING: TACKLING WHAT'S LEFT UNSAID

THE CAPACITY FOR TENSION

One of the most defining behaviors that distinguished the 10% of transformative leaders was their willingness to step into tension rather than retreat from it. Most leaders avoid confrontation, not due to a lack of awareness of the issues, but because they are reluctant to face the emotional discomfort associated with addressing them. They minimize micro-behaviors, dismiss subtle dysfunction, and rationalize avoidance by treating unresolved tensions as insignificant.

Yet, in every executive and leadership team I've worked with, those very behaviors—what was left unsaid, unchallenged, or unaddressed—were the invisible barriers to their highest performance. These micro-behaviors were small but significant. They were undermining collaboration, eroding trust, and creating friction that, over time, became embedded in the culture of the team.

In contrast, the 10% of leaders did something different. They understood that tension wasn't the issue; avoiding it was. In sessions, I often ask a simple but profound question: *"Before we leave today, what is being left unsaid?"*

Transformative leaders step forward. They are willing to tackle what had been quietly plaguing their teams for years. Their courage to confront allows them to bring hidden conflicts to the surface, dismantle barriers to progress, and resolve long-standing dynamics that have drained energy from their teams.

While it might seem simple in theory, in practice, confronting is one of the hardest behaviors for leadership teams to embrace. Confronting is the willingness to exert the energy to tackle the inconvenient, the uncomfortable, and the difficult. It involves creating space to handle the tension of tough discussions, both individually and within a team. It means addressing truths that have been ignored for years, even when doing so feels overwhelming or risky.

Confronting in action:

- **Naming**: Clearly identifying the issue, dynamic, or impact without blaming. It brings what's hidden to the surface so it can be addressed honestly. *"We've invested a lot into this direction, but it's clear it's not working the way we hoped."*

- **Entering**: Stepping into tension or turbulence with the intent to reach clarity, alignment, or resolution. *"This may feel uncomfortable, but we need to have this conversation if we're serious about moving forward together."*

- **Holding**: Staying in the discomfort long enough to let truth do its work—resisting the urge to retreat, deflect, or rush to closure before real understanding is reached. *"I know this is tense, but let's stay with it. There's something important here we haven't fully unpacked yet."*

EXAMPLE

During a leadership retreat, the team kept using semantics to avoid real decisions that would require accountability. The CEO finally paused and said:

"Every time we get to this subject, we keep getting into semantics which is delaying the ability to follow through."

That moment broke the pattern. What followed was uncomfortable but honest and marked the beginning of real accountability.

The courage to confront is not about conflict for conflict's sake. It is about addressing issues that have been avoided for years and taking a step towards it. It is a behavior rooted in courage, persistence, and a deep commitment to the truth in service of progress. Leaders who confront don't shy away from the hard truths; they meet them head-on, knowing that only by doing so can real change begin.

Confronting requires presence, courage, and a willingness to be moved.

TRANSPARENCY: THE BREAKTHROUGH CHARACTERISTIC

THE WILLINGNESS TO REVEAL TRUTH

Transparency is the opposite of managing image and is focused purely on impact. It means sharing truths that don't feel good: truths about the business, the strategy, the decision, or even the leader themselves. But it is precisely this kind of truth—uncomfortable and inconvenient—that reveals who a leader really is.

Transparency is the single most important characteristic because it determines whether power is used in service of purpose or in service of self-preservation. It separates exceptional leaders from those who allow ego, fear, or control to shape their decisions.

It is the foundation of excellence, the catalyst for meaningful productivity, and the cornerstone of the healthiest relationships. In organizations where transparency is practiced, truth is not filtered for optics or withheld to maintain control but honored, even when it disrupts.

Among the 10% of leaders who upheld their purpose, transparency was the defining factor that allowed every other behavior—vulnerability, humility, curiosity, and confronting—to flourish. It eliminated deception, eroded defensiveness, and created an environment where truth wasn't punished but actively sought. Transparency earned the highest level of credibility because when nothing was hidden, others could trust that nothing was distorted, influenced for personal gain, or concealed for control.

Leaders who practiced transparency understood that power is not in controlling one's image but in serving the collective good.

Transparency in action:

- **Revealing**: Openly sharing motives, reasoning, or information that affects others, even when it feels vulnerable or uncertain. *"I want to be clear about why this decision was made and what we were weighing behind the scenes—even if parts of it are still in motion."*

- **Declaring**: Naming information, needs, or decisions clearly and directly. It creates clarity and reduces the need for others to guess, assume, or interpret. *"I'm feeling frustrated, and what I need is a little patience while I work through this."*

- **Uncovering**: Bringing forward what has been concealed— whether emotions, information, or truths—so alignment and congruence can be restored. *"The numbers in this report aren't where we hoped they'd be—but I want to share them openly so we can understand what's behind them and address it together."*

In practice, transparency:

- Breaks through long-standing, unhealthy power dynamics and dramatically improves trust in decision-making.
- Dismantles the fear that keeps teams from speaking truth to leadership.
- Rebuilds trust where secrecy and avoidance had once eroded it.
- Shifts decision-making from self-protection to true alignment with purpose and impact.

Through transparency of truth, these leaders created a ripple effect that transformed their executive teams and their companies. Transparency enabled leaders and teams to act in the company's true best interest, balancing both profit and people for the first time. This shift was not just about sharing truths but about fostering a culture where those truths guided every decision, creating sustainable and meaningful progress.

> Transparency is the breakthrough characteristic because without it, transformation is impossible. It is the defining choice between preserving one's image or driving real change.

EXAMPLE

Mark was the chief operating officer of a successful, mid-sized company with approximately 3,000 employees. On paper, the organization was thriving—strong revenue, strong reputation, and continued growth. Mark's declared leadership purpose was this: *"To build a workplace where every voice is heard."* And he meant it, to his very core.

Until the anonymous employee survey.

The data revealed a different reality. It showed clear double standards in how leaders were treating employees—particularly based on who they favored or felt most comfortable with.

Certain employees were given more latitude, more visibility, and more grace, while others were more scrutinized and labeled as "difficult" when asking questions.

When I walked Mark through the findings, he grew quiet. Then he said, *"Don't share this with anyone."* He didn't elaborate. He redirected the conversation, and it was clear—the discussion was over. As a consultant, I advised otherwise, but I had to follow his direction. Because he had the power to bury it, he did. The report sat untouched.

Two months later, I was facilitating the company's executive offsite. It was day one. Someone raised their hand and asked, *"What are we doing about the employee survey?"*

The room fell silent. Mark and I locked eyes at the exact same moment. It's funny when I think about it now. It was one of those moments where everything slows down, like a movie scene, and the weight of the truth just hung there between us . . . I wanted to look away, tried to look away, but I couldn't.

And then, Mark stood up.

He took a breath and said, "I failed to act on what I knew because I didn't like what it said about me and others of us in this room. But I see that avoiding it is doing more damage. Let's talk about the survey today."

In that moment, Mark became part of the 10%. The 10% who choose principle over self-preservation in service of their purpose. He chose transparency of the truth as the path for progress.

That single decision set a new course for his leadership and for the organization. He released the report and invited the executive team into open, unfiltered conversation. He admitted their leadership had unintentionally contributed to patterns of exclusion and inequity, and he committed to doing better—publicly and repeatedly.

What followed wasn't performative. It was real. He changed how leadership meetings were run, who got invited to the table, how decisions were communicated, and how talent was evaluated. Were things perfect? No. Issues still arose, and problems still existed. But what changed was remarkable. Greater credibility. Higher trust. Stronger performance.

Mark didn't become a different person. He became a deeper, more honest version of the leader he had always aspired to be. And that's what transformative leadership looks like; not perfection, not performance, but the courage to confront what's hard and lead forward anyway.

THE POWER OF THE 5X5 FOR EVERY LEADER

This is the moment the work becomes personal.

You don't need a title to live this. And you don't need months to learn it. I've seen leaders shift how they show up overnight. Leaders who are adopting it are not only applying it in boardrooms, but in their living rooms. It's shifting how they listen and how they speak.

This is the discipline of power. And the 5x5 is the practice. It takes a moment. A pause. An interaction. A decision. That's why the leaders who adopt it often say, *"I can't unsee it anymore."* Because once you've seen the pattern, you see it everywhere—especially in yourself.

This is how power becomes principled. The kind of power that doesn't silence truth and instead makes room for it. The kind that doesn't protect your image, but protects the greater mission.

The 5x5 is the seed where transformation begins and is the foundation of the Transformation Formula. It bridges the gap between your purpose and your progress, helping you make choices that aren't driven by fear or ego, but on principle.

What makes this framework truly powerful is the 5x5 is for everyone. It's a mindset, a method, and a mirror. It doesn't just help you lead better. It helps you live better. And it's yours now.

7

CROSSING THE BRIDGE

As a leader, you are human. It's inevitable and natural to react from a place of ego. What matters is recognizing those reactions are betraying your purpose and understanding there is a way forward.

The 5x5 is not just a model, it's a bridge. Through my work, I identified that every ego-driven behavior on the left side has a corresponding solution on the right. It's like a prescription: a precise behavioral counter that helps you move from reaction to principle, from protection to purpose. These are not random opposites. They're the actual behavioral shifts the 10% made in moments that mattered. Each pattern on the right side of the 5x5 is a studied response—a precise, observable counter to the reactions that keep most leaders stuck.

For example, defensiveness isn't corrected by humility—it's disarmed by vulnerability. Impatience isn't overcome through confronting—it's tempered through curiosity.

Each of these gateways offers a path forward. And that bridge is what defines your leadership in the moment you encounter the dilemma, at the crossroads between ego and purpose.

This chapter will show you how to cross that bridge—again and again—during pivotal moments: when a hard truth has been shared, when a decision carries real consequences, or when the way you show up will either build trust or break it.

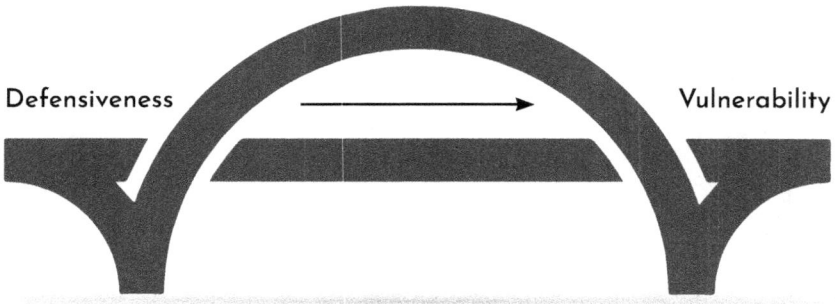

FROM DEFENSIVENESS TO VULNERABILITY

Vulnerability is the bridge from self-protection to self-awareness. The hardest part of this bridge is emotional, not intellectual. Defensiveness feels strong. It feels like control, conviction, even righteousness. That's why it's so seductive—it feels like strength when, in truth, it's a barrier to it. Vulnerability, by contrast, feels like weakness. It feels like exposure, uncertainty, and loss of footing. And yet, it's actually what power and strength looks like. This is your bridge to cross—the place where how you feel may be deceiving what is real.

EXAMPLE

In an organization where I was brought in to facilitate conflict mediation between senior leaders—as a preventive step before issues escalated into a formal HR matter—significant tensions had developed between racially diverse leaders. One particularly complex conflict involved a White male executive and a Black female senior director, following concerns about micro-invalidating communication in their interactions. The tension had been building for months.

He felt misunderstood and unfairly labeled, so his initial response was to defend himself—highlighting his support for her, his diverse upbringing, and his experience in multicultural environments. He was deeply offended, believing his intentions were being ignored. She, in turn, grew more frustrated, feeling that her concerns were being dismissed, her experience minimized, and felt more scrutinized and undermined.

During the conversation, something shifted—but it wasn't by accident. Both leaders had been trained on the 5x5 Framework and coached in advance on what it meant to sit in the "receiver chair"—to listen without defending, to acknowledge impact without deflection, and to remain open when discomfort arises. They both understood that resolution would require them not just to speak, but to receive.

He recognized his initial pull toward defensiveness and chose differently. He crossed the bridge toward vulnerability and stepped fully into the receiver chair. He listened. Truly listened.

The senior director shared how his tone and repeated questioning felt distrustful and punitive.

"I keep getting asked what I'm doing and where I'm at," she said. "It feels like you're assuming I'm not doing my job." These were lived experiences that had shaped her discomfort over time, subtle signals that accumulated and compounded into a sense of being unfairly scrutinized.

To his credit, he didn't interrupt to defend again. He acknowledged the impact of his communication style, even if his intent had been different. He owned how his approach could have been experienced through a lens he hadn't previously considered.

And then, she did something just as important: she moved into the receiver chair herself. She took in his feedback: that her response time to his emails was consistently slower than to others on the team; that she wasn't involving him as a thought partner on her projects the way her peers were; and that her collaboration with him was more limited. These weren't just perceptions; they were observable patterns that had created a sense of exclusion on his end and raised concerns about alignment.

Together, we explored not only the behavioral styles illuminated by the DISC profiles, but also the racial, gender, and cultural dynamics that were silently shaping their interactions. At the same time, we named the level of responsiveness, partnership, and collaboration needed for a healthy, trusting relationship.

It wasn't about proving who was right. It was about uncovering what was real for each of them. And once they both saw it—without defensiveness—that's when the conversation shifted from conflict to clarity. And for the first time, a path forward was made possible.

HOW TO MOVE FROM DEFENSIVE TO VULNERABILITY

Ask, *What am I protecting*? Is your reaction about preserving your identity, avoiding discomfort, or remaining guarded?

Focus on impact, not intent: Acknowledge impact, admit blind spots, and recognize where you may have made a misstep.

Feel it: If it feels weak, realize it's actually strength. Show your team by saying, "I hear you. I see where I can improve. Let's work on this together." Owning growth builds trust.

What feels like weakness is actually the birthplace of strength. Vulnerability isn't the absence of power—it's the presence of it. It is one of the rarest, rawest expressions of courage in leadership. When a leader chooses to listen instead of defend, to receive instead of rationalize, they are not backing down—they are stepping up. To be vulnerable in the moments that matter is to hold the weight of responsibility and still be willing to be reshaped by truth.

That is not fragility. That is strength in its most honest form.

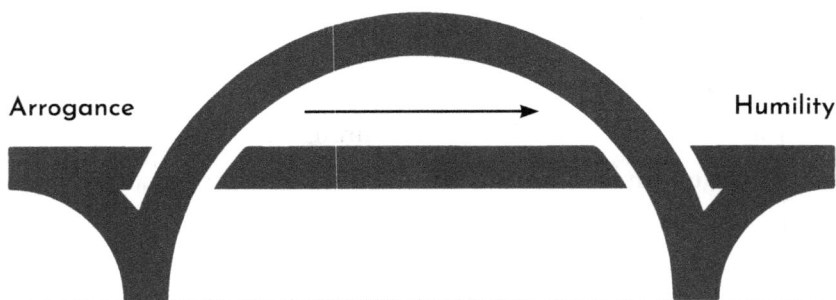

Arrogance ⟶ Humility

FROM ARROGANCE TO HUMILITY

The hardest part of crossing this bridge is pride.

Humility is moving from your preferences to practicing receptivity. Pride convinces you that stepping back is stepping down. It tells you that asking for input will weaken your authority, that acknowledging someone else's expertise will undermine your own. It makes collaboration feel like compromise, and self-awareness feel like surrender.

**Pride convinces you that you're right
rather than searching for what is right.**

But this is the shift: moving from pride to humility is not about giving up confidence or power—it's about giving up the need to prove it.

EXAMPLE

In one of my recent workshops, I met a hospital department manager who found herself in ongoing conflict with a nurse who frequently brought concerns to the union. The manager, feeling frustrated and under scrutiny, believed the nurse was simply being difficult and overly combative. Convinced she was in the right, she held firm in her authority. She assumed that if the nurse would just follow procedures, everything would run more smoothly.

Applying the 5x5 Framework, the manager recognized how she may be conveying an air of superiority. Rather than insisting on her own expertise or reinforcing the chain of command, she took a step in humility: she asked the nurse for input on how to improve the implementation of a patient care policy that had been facing resistance.

The response was surprising. The nurse provided practical insights, which the manager incorporated into the revised rollout. The department saw greater compliance with the policy, and tension between the two began to ease. The manager later reflected on how the experience had an impact not just on her professional life, but her personal life too. She stopped leading from her own preferences and became more open to others.

By inviting expertise from someone other than herself, the manager created trust, improved outcomes, and modeled a more inclusive, collaborative way forward.

Leadership isn't shown in dominance, it's found in restraint. What they gain is greater efficacy in the result itself.

HOW TO MOVE FROM ARROGANCE TO HUMILITY

Challenge your default assumptions: Ask yourself, *"Am I prioritizing what I prefer, or what's truly the best way forward?"* This forces you to confront blind spots and expand your thinking.

Credit others' contributions: Proactively credit others for their contributions in your decisions and results. Arrogance dissolves when you recognize the collective effort over your individual role.

Practice shifting the focus outward instead of inward: It's expressed by listening, seeking collaboration, and approaching projects, situations, or decisions in ways that reflect the collective good rather than your individual preference.

Humility is not insecurity. It's self-discipline. When pride is set aside, what remains is a leader others can follow, not because they have to, but because they want to.

Crossing the bridge from arrogance to humility begins when you stop being the smartest person in the room and start appreciating the intelligence and contributions of those around you.

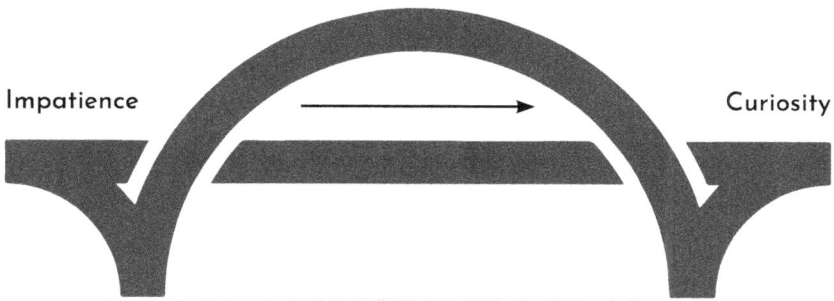

FROM IMPATIENCE TO CURIOSITY

Curiosity interrupts the impulse to oversimplify. The hardest part of crossing this bridge is recognizing that slowing down isn't falling behind; it's setting up for acceleration that actually lasts. Most leaders don't fail because they don't act fast enough; they fail because they act without seeing the whole picture.

EXAMPLE

Mariella, a finance director known for her efficiency and results-driven leadership, had great success around taking swift action. Her default approach in team meetings was direct and transactional: deliver information, assign next steps, and move on. With limited time and a full calendar, she saw extended dialogue as inefficient.

But over time, her impatience began to erode trust within her team, particularly in the finance department, which was already experiencing tension. Team members felt dismissed, misunderstood, and wary of her conclusions. The fast pace was leading to misinterpretations, rushed judgments, and decisions made with little to no context.

After being introduced to the 5x5 Framework, Mariella began to see the cost of her urgency. She recognized that her instinct to simplify complex situations wasn't serving the team or her leadership. With intentional effort, she began to lead differently. In meetings, instead of rushing to provide answers, she started asking more questions. She paused to gather context before making decisions and gave space for her team to offer insights that she hadn't considered.

This shift toward curiosity didn't slow progress—it accelerated it. By investing time on the front end during group discussions and strategy sessions, the department saw a significant culture shift in just three months. Trust was rebuilt. Outcomes improved. Even difficult personnel decisions were handled with greater objectivity and care.

Mariella learned that curiosity isn't a fixed personality trait. It is a strategic skill. Slowing down to ask better questions led to faster alignment, deeper insight, and more effective decisions.

HOW TO MOVE FROM IMPATIENCE TO CURIOSITY

Identify the pressure: Ask yourself, *"What's driving my urgency? Is it the actual situation, or my discomfort with waiting?"* Recognizing the source of impatience helps you slow down.

Reframe inactivity as inquiry: Bring your team into the conversation and ask, *"What am I missing?"* or *"Is there another way to approach this?"* Inviting diverse perspectives slows the rush to conclusions and opens up new possibilities.

See efficacy as efficiency: Ask, *"What decision here will create the greatest long-term value?"*

Remember, you're not delaying progress. You're creating conditions for sustainable and intentional acceleration.

Crossing this bridge means letting go of urgency and choosing depth over speed. It's one of the most disciplined forms of leadership—and one of the most transformative.

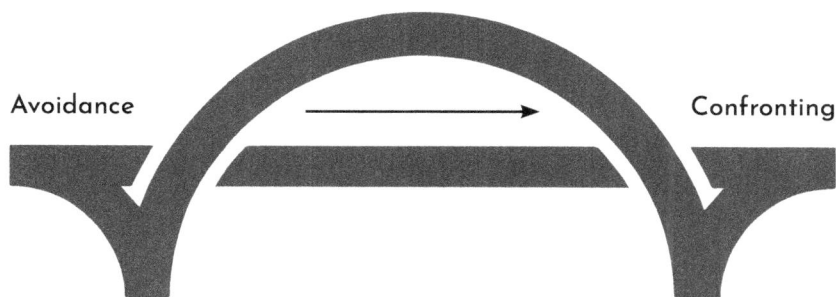

Avoidance ⟶ Confronting

FROM AVOIDANCE TO CONFRONTING

The most difficult part of this bridge is realizing that harmony isn't the same as honesty—and getting honest about that is where the real work begins. Many leaders mistake the absence of tension for alignment, when in truth, what's left unspoken is often what's holding everything back. Confronting isn't about being combative. It's about being courageous enough to engage with emotional discomfort and tension. Healthy confronting in leadership means addressing the difficult truths, the unspoken issues, and the sensitive dynamics others often avoid. It's choosing progress over preservation, even when it costs you comfort.

EXAMPLE

In two different organizations I worked with, internal culture change groups were formed with the goal of addressing systemic issues and improving workplace culture. Both groups reached a similar point of being faced with uncomfortable truths. How the leadership of each organization responded revealed the profound difference between avoiding and confronting.

In the first organization, it took months to build enough psychological safety for members to speak honestly about their experiences. When they finally did, the result was a breakthrough conversation. Frustration turned into energy. The group moved from resignation to re-engagement, feeling hopeful and ready to be part of the solution. But when the meeting was shared with the executive team, the response was swift and fearful: the leader facilitating the group was let go, and the entire group was disbanded.

Leadership labeled the group as "off-mission" and claimed it had lost focus but in reality, they were avoiding the discomfort of truth. Rather than engaging with what was said, they shut it down. The result was a deep loss of trust. People left the organization. Those who stayed never looked at leadership the same way again. The potential for progress was traded for the comfort of silence.

In the second organization, this group also surfaced difficult truths: perceptions of favoritism, inequitable treatment, and protected status for certain individuals. But instead of retreating, leadership chose to confront these issues head-on. They acknowledged the findings and listened as employees expressed their concerns. They didn't pretend the situation was easy. But they committed to doing the work.

This path wasn't comfortable. People had to name feelings they'd been avoiding, speak candidly to colleagues, and risk tension with their leaders. But because they confronted the truth together, gossip diminished, blame shifted to collaboration, and the team began making real progress. Trust started to rebuild. Most importantly, the leadership was willing to walk through discomfort. Confronting, in this case, created a path forward.

Both organizations faced a similar challenge. One avoided it and lost momentum, credibility, and people. The other confronted it and moved toward healing and change. The difference was in how leadership responded when truth came to the table.

HOW TO MOVE FROM AVOIDANCE TO CONFRONTING

Name what's being avoided: Start by identifying the specific tension, behavior, or truth that's being sidestepped whether in a relationship, a meeting, or a decision. Avoidance thrives in vagueness. Naming it gives it form, and once it has form, it can be addressed.

Shift from harmony to honesty: Let go of the need to preserve comfort as the highest goal.

Commit to the truth: Confronting requires commitment to truth, even when it's uncomfortable. Emotional resilience means staying with the process, reminding yourself, *"The cost of ignoring this is greater than the discomfort of addressing it."*

The breakthrough happens just after the moment you most want to retreat. Healthy and respectful confronting isn't only directed outward—it's also deeply internal. It requires you to reflect honestly on how you may be contributing to what you want improved upon.

Crossing the bridge from avoidance to confronting is about cultivating the emotional stamina to move from the illusion of peace to the power of truth.

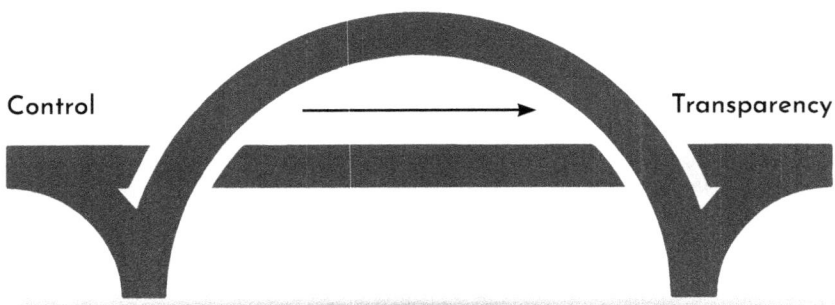

Control → Transparency

FROM CONTROL TO TRANSPARENCY

The biggest bridge to cross here is moving from protecting to revealing—from managing perception to serving the purpose. Control can feel like a valid form of caution but it masks what's really happening: protection of self or someone you care about above everything else.

A critical part of this bridge is moving from *me* to *us*. Control is inherently individual—it centers on what *I* need to manage, what *I* fear will be exposed, what *I* want to maintain. Transparency expands the focus to the collective—what *we* need to understand, what *we* need to face, and what *we* must solve together.

EXAMPLE

An executive I was coaching had built her leadership style around control. She carefully managed information, limited access to data, and made key decisions in isolation. She believed she was protecting the company and shielding it from greater legal ramifications.

She wasn't acting in bad faith. She believed that concealing sensitive information was the responsible choice. That transparency might create liability, invite misinterpretation, or spark unnecessary conflict. In her mind, withholding was a form of stewardship.

Over time, she began to see what control was actually costing: trust, alignment, and long-term credibility. Through applying the 5x5 Framework, she started to recognize the unintended consequences. Together, we unpacked the fear beneath the behavior. She was afraid that revealing too much could be used against her, or worse, against the company.

So, she began to practice. Slowly. At first, it was just naming the fear. Then, it was talking through the risks out loud, imagining worst-case scenarios and asking whether control was truly reducing harm or simply delaying it.

The turning point came when she and the leadership team made the decision to share previously restricted data on employee terminations—specifically patterns related to tenure, age, race, and gender. Instead of keeping it hidden, for the first time, the executives examined the disparities together. Leaders didn't leave with all the answers, but they left with something more powerful: ownership.

That executive will tell you it's still uncomfortable. But she's building the muscle. She's learning that transparency isn't about exposure for its own sake; it's about revealing the truths that matter, in the right context, to build trust, address root causes, and lead forward with integrity.

And now she knows: what she thought was protection was actually prevention. Prevention of change. Prevention of trust. Prevention of progress.

HOW TO MOVE FROM CONTROL TO TRANSPARENCY

Acknowledge the fear: Ask yourself, "What am I afraid of revealing, and why?" Reframe your mindset by asking, "How can revealing this truth benefit the team, the organization, or the greater good?" This shifts the focus from self-preservation to service.

Start small, be strategic: Transparency does not mean oversharing; it means responsible and strategic honesty. Identify what truth needs to be shared, why it matters, and how it serves the greater purpose.

Share truth within right context: Context builds psychological safety, and transparency works when framed with care. Be clear about why you're sharing, what's known, what's unknown, and what you're asking of others. This models responsibility, not recklessness.

Transparency shifts the weight from *I must fix this* to *we must face this*. Invite others into the process to build trust through co-leadership. This is where the bridge from me to us is fully crossed. Ask, "Now that we know this, what do we want to do about it, together?"

PRACTICAL GUIDANCE AS YOU CROSS THE BRIDGES

As a leader, you will face defining moments—those crossroads where you must choose between the path of least resistance and the path of great resistance. One offers comfort, convenience, and control. The other asks more of you. It asks you to let go of certainty, to confront tension, and to act with principle when others need you to place service above self.

It's in these moments that the **5x5 Framework** becomes your guide. It grounds you when pressure tempts you to compromise. It reorients you when ego wants to take the lead. And it gives language, structure, and direction to the most difficult moments of your leadership—when doing what's right risks more than staying silent.

When you feel yourself hesitating to speak or hear the truth, delaying a hard decision, or rationalizing control in the name of safety—pause. Those are not signs of weakness. They're signals that a bridge is in front of you. One you are meant to cross.

Lean into the 5x5. Let it stretch you. Let it challenge you. The more you work with it, the more it becomes a part of how you think, speak, and lead. Like any form of strength, it grows with use and what once felt like a heavy lift will one day become second nature.

When leaders cross these bridges—openly, honestly, and repeatedly—they don't just grow. They become unshaken. So lean into the resistance. Let the resistance be opportunities to refine you.

The world doesn't need perfect leaders. It needs unshaken ones—those who choose purpose over preservation and truth over comfort. Your courage becomes the catalyst that turns resistance into progress and leadership into legacy.

8

THE DISRUPTIVE NATURE
OF TRANSFORMATIVE
LEADERSHIP

As you step into transformative leadership, there's an important thing to share: this *is* the path of greater resistance. This path is not the simplest or easiest; it will test your will, and what you do will reveal what truly matters to you. It forces honesty; first with yourself, then with others. This journey will include loss and at times may feel isolating, but know that it leads to an internal sense of peace and confidence that no title or achievement alone can offer.

Understanding what lies ahead is essential so you don't give up or give in.

Many organizations want innovation, inclusion, and an inspiring vision, but when progress requires disruption, tackling roadblocks, or doing things differently, they retreat to what's familiar and easy. The desire for change is real, but the commitment to what change requires is where most stop short. By stepping into transformative leadership, you challenge these ingrained behaviors, which can make those around you resist in different ways, in self-protective ways.

This disapproval does not signal poor leadership, as long as you're leading without superiority, judgment, or contempt. Unwavering principles in service of the bigger mission will disrupt systems that have traditionally depended on compromise, hierarchy, or surface-level efforts.

Your actions can and will ignite transformation in any environment, strengthen every relationship, and redefine what is possible in any business.

The key? To disrupt in the least disruptive way. This is critical. You must be collaborative, cooperative, and consensus focused.

Your role? To stay the course.

WHAT YOUR PRESENCE PROVOKES

People's reactions will vary. Some will respect your commitment to this growth and impact while others may resist, misinterpret, or even challenge your actions because they cannot yet see who they aren't ready to become. This is because many individuals are accustomed to loyalty being tied to relationships rather than principles. As a transformative, purpose-driven leader, you shift the focus from personal allegiance to alignment with values for the greater good—a distinction that can be difficult for others to recognize.

LOYALTY TO A PERSON VS. LOYALTY TO A PRINCIPLE

Relationships are vital to our lives. Be cautious of those who require loyalty at the expense of your principles and purpose. Loyalty to a person often carries unspoken expectations: silent agreements to overlook, excuse, or stay silent in service of the relationship, even when it conflicts with what should be done. When obedience is a condition, it moves you out of integrity and into protection.

Loyalty to a principle, on the other hand, anchors you in your purpose. It demands that you prioritize what serves the greater mission, even when it challenges those closest to you.

The strongest relationships are those that can withstand the truth spoken in service to the shared good of the whole.

Being people-centered is powerful when it brings out the best in ourselves and others, but never mistake it as requiring obedience.

I once faced this when a committee member who had voted to award me a contract, later expected my endorsement of her actions in a conflict with leadership. She demanded my personal loyalty over my professional insight. The executive team was already making decisions based on personal alliances rather than strategy or mission-centered reasons—exactly the dynamic I was helping them dismantle. I had to make a choice: maintain her favor or remain principled and address the issue objectively.

I chose the latter. As a result, she and her friends cut ties with me, which had the potential for professional ramifications in this tight-knit industry. Though there was personal loss and professional risk, there was never any doubt or hesitation about what the right decision was.

But here's the critical point: this moment posed a real dilemma. It could have been a difficult decision. Because my principles were clear, there was no internal conflict. My loyalty to principle ensured I stayed steady and true to the responsibility of my role, where my guidance and judgment were being relied upon. The short-term loss was necessary for the long-term health of the organization—and my own integrity.

TRUTH AT THE CROSSROADS: THE PIVOTAL MOMENTS

Truth rarely arrives gently. It disrupts. It unsettles. And for leaders in positions of power, it often feels like a threat. It challenges stability, image, privilege, or the illusion of control.

Power protects the comfortable.
Truth protects the necessary.

In the introduction, the three greatest threats were outlined that caused 90% of purpose-driven leaders to abandon the greater mission when discomfort surfaced. Now, we return to those threats but through the lens of truth as the catalyst.

These three forms of truth that consistently shake people in power offer information—and they surface tension, stir resistance, and bring you to a choice point.

The question is not *if* these truths will show up. The question is: what will you do *when they do?*

TRUTH SPOKEN WHEN YOU'RE IN POWER

When someone with less formal power or less favorable currency challenges a decision, dynamic, or behavior, it can feel like disrespect instead of insight. For many leaders, upward or lateral truth triggers defensiveness, not reflection. This isn't because the feedback is necessarily inaccurate, but it may expose unexpected blind spots.

Examples:

- Someone raises concerns about inconsistent performance metrics being used to evaluate different departments.
- A business partner questions whether current investments align with long-term growth objectives, pushing for a data-driven course correction.
- A colleague highlights the gap between the organization's stated values and the KPIs being prioritized.
- An analyst challenges the strategic direction in a planning meeting, presenting overlooked data that contradicts the current trajectory.

TRUTH THAT CONTRADICTS HOW YOU SEE YOURSELF

Few things are more threatening than a truth that disrupts your identity as a leader. When you see yourself as inclusive, ethical, or fair and someone discusses a lived experience that contradicts that, it creates internal dissonance. The instinct is to reject the truth to protect the self-image.

Examples:

- A leader known for being "people-first" is told they're micromanaging and condescending in their communication.
- A champion for diversity, equity, and inclusion is informed their behavior is marginalizing and alienating others.
- A respected decision-maker learns their leadership style is intimidating or controlling.
- An advocate for innovation is told their approach silences dissent and rushes implementation without alignment.

TRUTH THAT EXPOSES OR PERCEIVES INEQUITY

When patterns of favoritism, bias, or systemic advantage are made visible, those who benefit often feel the ground shift beneath them.

Whether the inequity is real or perceived, the exposure challenges the belief the system is fair or success is fully merit-based.

Examples:

- A firm partner receives feedback they're consistently assigning high-visibility and higher-earning projects to one associate, raising concerns about fairness.
- A high performer points out that relationships—not performance—decides opportunities.
- Data reveals disparities in promotion or pay based on race, gender, or background.
- An executive is seen as enforcing double standards by holding some team members accountable while excusing others for similar behavior.

Each of these moments of perceived or real truth carries weight. When they surface, there are people who are looking to you to both acknowledge the inequity and take some type of action. Your action, guided by principle, is not risk free.

Speaking up, rebalancing opportunity, or holding everyone to the same standard can cost political capital, stability, even personal security. Yet improvement cannot begin until someone is willing to take that risk. The following are the most common risks the 10% of transformative leaders face when principle pushes them to do the right thing, and guidance on how to navigate those risks without abandoning the very purpose you set out to serve.

THE FIVE RISKS OF TRANSFORMATIVE LEADERSHIP

Here's what I've noticed as an unavoidable pattern: the risk and the sacrifice come first. The reward: it comes after and later . . . but have faith that it does arrive.

This is why principles are the key ingredient that keep you anchored to your purpose. What caused the 90% of leaders whom I studied to abandon their purpose wasn't a lack of care or commitment—it was that safety was prioritized. The risk felt too great, and they couldn't see past the potential sacrifice or loss.

The human brain is wired to protect. Neuroscience tells us that when we anticipate a risk—whether it's status, influence, approval, or security—the amygdala activates our threat response. The brain becomes hyper-focused on short-term survival rather than long-term vision. This makes it neurologically difficult to imagine a future reward when immediate discomfort or reputational risk is in front of us.

But transformative leadership requires exactly that: faith in a future you can't yet see. You have to lead through the loss before you experience the gain.

Let this be your reminder: you are not being tested because you're on the wrong path. You're being tested because you're on the right one. And these five risks? They aren't signs to stop. They are the very proof that transformation is underway.

RISK OF SACRIFICE

Let's start with a hard truth: you may lose people or opportunities along the way. Leading with uncompromised principles to serve a higher mission will mean losing friendships, business relationships, contracts, or even jobs. You may find yourself at a crossroads where someone expects you to prioritize loyalty to them over your values, and when you don't, the relationship might not survive.

And when the sacrifice is made for the sake of others—for those with less voice, less safety, or less power—it can feel especially devastating when those very people go silent.

When you disrupt the status quo to protect others, you likely won't be celebrated. You may not be thanked. In fact, what you often get in return is isolation. Why? Because the people who witnessed the fallout—the consequence of your courage—are now scared. They see what standing up can cost. And instead of joining you, many will step back to protect themselves.

Some will do it quietly. Others will pretend they didn't see what happened. And yes, even those who once counted on your voice, who relied on you to say what they couldn't—may go quiet the moment you need them most. It's a hard truth, and a hard moment. But it's one that every transformative leader must walk through.

This is the heartbreak of sacrifice: you don't just lose something tangible—you lose the belief that others will always show up when you do.

Coaching tip: When you do the right thing, there will be no applause, no immediate validation—and that's exactly when your ego may need it the most. Your emotional resilience depends on this one truth: you must be so grounded in your purpose that your affirmation comes from within. You have to know—without hesitation—that you would make the same decision again, no matter what it cost you. The integrity of your choice is what gives you the energy to keep going.

RISK OF BACKLASH

Let's address a hard reality: challenging dysfunction, pushing for change, and disrupting the status quo can take on a more personal and more dangerous form. This is the risk of backlash. And when it comes from someone in a position of power—your supervisor, a senior leader, or someone who controls access and influence—it doesn't just sting. It can shake your sense of safety.

Backlash can show up in three covert but damaging forms:

- **Sabotage disguised as oversight**: Your work is quietly altered or stripped of visibility under the guise of "realignment."

- **Character assassination framed as concern**: Offhand comments or subtle doubts about your temperament, "fit," or approach are seeded into leadership conversations.

- **Discrediting masked as feedback**: Comments are made about your work that chip away at your credibility such as subtle remarks in meetings, offhand critiques, or reframing your contributions in ways that diminish their value. These aren't based on valid concerns; they're delivered as a consequence. It's framed as feedback, but functions as retaliation altering how others perceive you while protecting the person delivering it.

A senior compliance manager was asked by a company executive to backdate documentation tied to an internal audit. Doing so would have violated both regulatory standards and the organization's own reporting policies. He declined—professionally and with clear reasoning—stating that it would put him out of compliance and compromise the integrity of the process.

What followed was a quiet but deliberate effort to discredit him. Comments were made in meetings questioning his judgment. His decision-making was reframed as inflexible. His alignment with leadership was called into question. None of it reflected his actual performance. It was a consequence for refusing to do something unethical.

He had previously been viewed as a trusted, capable leader respected for his prudence and thoroughness. But after that moment, the tone around him began to shift. Slowly, his reputation was chipped away, not by anything he did wrong but by how others were led to reinterpret his leadership.

Coaching tip: When the backlash comes from above, your character holds you steady. Assert your integrity with humility, absent of superiority, self-righteousness, or judgment. Calm, consistent truth-telling may not disrupt sabotage but it will preserve your credibility and protect your integrity long after.

If you weren't making a difference, no one would resist you. It's also a powerful sign that you're leading in the right direction.

RISK OF ECONOMIC SECURITY

Let's get real about the risk of jeopardizing your financial stability. Fulfilling your purpose by standing firm in your principles becomes incredibly difficult when it threatens your promotion, business contracts, compensation, or overall career. When your income supports bills, mortgages, families, and futures, the pressure to conform doesn't feel optional; it feels necessary.

The 10% of transformative leaders weren't part of the 1%. They didn't have generational wealth, unlimited resources, or financial privilege to cushion the impact. They weren't protected. They were fully exposed to the consequences. In every company, power sits with one or two select individuals who can withhold contracts, terminate employment, prevent opportunities, or exclude you from future opportunities. This does happen.

But here's what those individuals can't take away: the respect, trust, and credibility earned from the people who witnessed the truth. The majority may stay silent in the moment—but they are watching. They remember who stood firm. And while financial loss is real, it's also temporary.

That trust becomes your reputation and that outlasts any paycheck. The money will come again, often in greater amounts and from better-aligned opportunities. What can't be bought or replaced is who you became in the process.

Coaching tip: Don't make a short-term decision that violates who you are just to protect what you might lose. Integrity and efficacy don't just preserve your credibility—they protect your future.

Now I know, many of you may be thinking right now, *Forget this. My paycheck comes first.* And I get that. I've been in that exact place. And when the stakes are financial, it's scary as hell. But hear me clearly: this isn't theory! It's truth I've lived myself and truth the 10% of leaders have experienced time and again.

At the beginning of this book, I shared the story that led me to start my consulting company—when I was let go as Vice President after attempting to improve our team's workplace culture. These were people who consistently went above and beyond, not occasionally, but as a way of being. There was no psychological safety because the power hierarchy was strongly imposed. (And this was before the term *psychological safety* was even named or understood.)

I assured them they could be honest about how they were being treated and that I wouldn't let them lose their jobs for it. What I didn't know was they had already asked themselves: *What if she loses hers for standing for us?* It wasn't something I had considered. But it happened.

They resigned—after giving the CEO an operational handbook with all passwords, logins, and files. All of them quit. No backup jobs. No financial safety nets. They walked away with nothing but their final paycheck—on principle.

Each of them landed on their feet. They didn't just move up in title, they continually rose in their careers and are now thriving in both their lives and in who they've become.

We learned the CEO had spread falsehoods that could have sabotaged all our chances of being hired. I worried I wouldn't find work because we stayed silent and let those lies stand. Yet I signed contracts with a Global Fortune 20 and a privately held, multimillion-dollar company operating across multiple states, launching the beginning of my firm.

Years later, I reunited us on a large scale project I led that earned us the Diversity Excellence Award in North America.

The short-term cost was real. The long-term reward both professionally and personally, tenfold.

I share this to offer hope—to encourage you and to give you confidence. So when that moment comes, you'll choose what aligns with who you are, not what fear pushes you to do.

So whether it's prayer, meditation, faith in a higher power, or simply a return to your purpose—hold onto what steadies you. Make the decision you'll still be proud of five years from now. The right opportunities will find their way back to those who didn't lose themselves trying to keep them. I believe this for you because I've lived it time and again.

RISK OF EMOTIONAL TOLL

Now let's talk about the emotional weight. After the sacrifice, after the backlash, and after the financial hit what's left is you, alone with the emotional cost. It takes a toll; it takes stamina and over time it can wear you down.

Losing opportunities, income, work, and relationships is a hard pill to swallow. But what makes it heavier is when no one acknowledges what it cost you to do the right thing. It can feel like you're standing on an island, holding the weight of everyone else's silence and wondering if you should've stayed quiet, too.

When you've arrived here, it can shake you. It can make you question yourself, your higher calling, even your value. Worse, it can harden you. It feels easier to sit in a place of resignation, to protect yourself by pulling back, operating from self-interest, or deciding not to care as much next time. And that's when ego wins—and purpose loses.

Coaching tip: Take a break—but don't take a detour. Rest. Regroup. This is when your support system matters most. Pick up the phone. Schedule the walk. Say yes to the invitation. Whether it's cocktails with a colleague, a round of golf with your foursome, or a simple text to a friend who's walked this road before, refuel with people who know your path and honor your mission. They're not just your relief, they're your reminder.

RISK OF DELAYED RESULTS

We must face that we want progress, and we want it now. We live in a world that moves fast, rewards speed, and pressures leaders to keep up. For high-performing, competitive leaders, slowing down can feel like falling behind. And when you're used to delivering quick wins, one of the greatest risks in transformative leadership is the fear that things aren't moving fast enough.

The real work—the work that changes culture, mindset, systems, and outcomes—takes more effort, more resources, and more time . . . upfront. And that feels risky.

However, by trying to move faster, leaders actually waste more time, spend more money, and become more fatigued. The frustrating irony? You end up back in the same place—only now with more criticism and less credibility.

If you are doing change right, you will have delayed results but that doesn't mean failure—it means you're slowing down to accelerate. The only way to advance the performance of your company is by going deeper before going faster.

Transformative leadership is similar to the scar removal process. Just as laser treatments require multiple sessions, precise targeting, and time for the skin to heal and regenerate, real change happens in layers, through a series of intentional, methodical steps. The first treatment doesn't erase the scar. It triggers a process beneath the surface, gradually breaking down old tissue and stimulating renewal. Skipping steps or rushing the process doesn't accelerate healing; it increases the risk of damage and ineffective results.

Transformative leadership is measured by endurance and courage—not speed.

Coaching tip: Give it six months to do the real work, the deeper work. If you can hold steady—resist shortcuts and stay consistent— you will see meaningful results start to emerge within three months.

Real progress compounds, but only if you're willing to be patient on the front end.

Before you cave to urgency, ask yourself this: *Do I want visible results next month that don't last or do I want real outcomes six months from now that won't unravel?*

Commit to the long game. The upfront investment of time, energy, and patience is far less expensive than the long-term price of cutting corners. It's the difference between buying cheap and replacing it often or building it right once and letting it last.

THE COST OF LEADING BY A CODE

Imagine seeing what others choose to ignore. You notice unhealthy patterns of behavior quietly eroding trust, morale, and performance. Maybe it's a high performer whose impact is harmful. Maybe it's a dynamic everyone works around but no one addresses.

The easy path is concealment. To tell yourself it's not your role, that it's not worth the disruption, or to hope it resolves on its own. But when you lead by a code—when you've committed to something greater than comfort—courage demands more.

I coached a leader in this exact situation. She knew confronting the issue would cause friction. She feared the political consequences, the personal backlash, and what it might jeopardize her relationships. But she also knew that ignoring it would cost the team more.

So she chose the harder path. She brought the team together, named the behavior that had gone unspoken, acknowledged its impact, and set a new standard. The room was tense. The moment was uncomfortable. But it was real. And it was the turning point. Trust began to rebuild. People exhaled. Accountability started to take root—not because of what was fixed, but because someone finally stopped pretending it wasn't broken.

Courage isn't comfortable but it's what turns leadership from performative to transformative. Anyone can spot dysfunction. Few will disrupt it. The cost of leading by a code is real but so is the change it creates.

THE MOUNT EVEREST ANALOGY

I use the analogy of climbing Mount Everest to describe the intense challenges leaders face when navigating cultural transformation. Just as climbers must pass through Everest's perilous "death zone"—where oxygen is insufficient, conditions are brutal, and the margin for error is razor-thin—leaders must also enter their own organizational death zones: moments where inequity, favoritism, and consequences for speaking the truth threaten progress.

Every year, thousands of climbers attempt Everest, guided by Sherpas who have mastered the terrain. Leaders often see themselves as those Sherpas—guiding others through complexity with clarity and confidence. But the truth is, leaders are also the climbers, unsure if they'll make it through, and bearing the weight of every decision as they ascend with their teams.

In the death zone, progress is slow. Breathing gets harder. Stagnation creeps in. Turning back feels like the safest option. And yet, climbers know: to reach the summit they must go through the death zone. It's the hardest part—but also the most defining.

The same is true in transformation. When the pressure is highest and the resistance strongest, it's not a sign to retreat, it's proof you're close. The death zone in leadership is where most give up but it's also where the breakthrough happens.

What is your mountain? What change or transformation are you trying to lead that feels big, daunting, or worth the climb?

Where is your death zone? What part of the journey feels the most exhausting, risky, or where you're tempted to quit?

What is your oxygen? What keeps you going when the pressure rises—your purpose, your people, your faith, or something else?

THE PAIN BEFORE THE REWARD

Stepping into transformative, purpose-driven leadership will not only feel like an uphill battle, it will be one. Loss, consequence, and sacrifices are inevitable. True transformation demands endurance. The death zone will test everything in you: your values, your resolve, your tolerance for risk.

But it's also the stretch right before the summit. The question isn't whether the journey will be hard—it will be. The real question is this: Are you willing to endure the pain that comes before the reward? Because your reward is transformation, unfolding with every step you take forward and every choice not to turn back.

9

THE REWARDS OF BEING TRANSFORMATIVE

Growing up, we had a big garden in the backyard and several flower beds that stretched across the front. Our summers weren't spent sleeping in—we worked. Every morning, before anything else, we were out in the garden and in the flower beds pulling weeds. That was only half of our chores. If we wanted anything to grow—if we wanted to see flowers bloom or food on the table—we had to take care of the ground it came from.

I didn't enjoy it at all. I didn't like getting up early. I didn't like the dirt under my nails or being out in the heat all day doing these chores. But if we didn't do it, the garden wouldn't produce and the flowers wouldn't grow.

Because we maintained them, they flourished. The vegetables multiplied. The flowers bloomed. We had fresh food from the garden at dinner nearly every night. We enjoyed fresh fruit when it was in season. We could see beautiful flowers across the yard and fresh-cut tulips in our home. Our garden grew so much that we'd give away baskets of vegetables and fruit to neighbors, church friends, and anyone who needed them. But it only grew because we maintained it.

When we fell behind, the weeds reminded us.

They didn't take over all at once. They crept in—small at first, then spreading, and eventually taking root. The more we missed them, because we were going too fast (because the faster we got done the quicker we could maybe go out and play), the deeper they grew and it took more work to pull them. They would get rooted in deeply and not only get harder to pull but also risked damaging what was good around them. Maintenance became recovery.

And the same thing happens in organizations.

Unaddressed truth in a culture behaves just like weeds. It starts small—something someone said, favoring "me" above "we," a pattern people quietly work around. It doesn't seem urgent, so it gets ignored. But over time, it spreads.

The real weeds in your culture aren't the big, visible events like a layoff or a policy failure. They're subtle issues and micro-behaviors. The daily dynamics that go unspoken: such as dismissing, exclusion, or discrediting. Because they're small, they're easy to dismiss. But that's what makes them dangerous.

What I've found is that the micro issues are actually the most significant. They are the thistles of your culture—deep-rooted, slow to show their damage, and hard to pull once they've taken hold. The longer they're left alone, the more they entangle themselves in how people communicate, how decisions get made, and how power operates.

Unfavorable truth. Unpleasant truth. Uncomfortable truth. These are the weeds. They take more effort. More time. More emotional labor. But skipping over them always costs more in the long run.

Transformative leaders don't just focus on what they want to grow—they pay attention to what's getting in the way. They pull the weeds while they're still small. They stay close enough to the ground to notice the early signs of toxicity. They understand that maintaining a healthy, high-performing culture requires ongoing attention to the smallest signals, because those are what scale—either in service to your values or in conflict with them.

THE ORGANIZATIONAL REWARDS

When leaders choose to be transformative, the culture doesn't just improve; it unlocks a higher level of performance. The organization begins to operate with clarity, energy, and efficacy. People want to stay. Talent becomes loyal—not because of perks, but because of purpose. And what once felt stuck begins to move with power and precision.

Here's what that looks like:

- **Healthy power dynamics** – In transformative cultures, power isn't protected or politicized—it's earned. Influence comes through demonstrated competence, consistent contribution, and alignment with shared values, not proximity to authority or personal loyalty. Decisions reflect what serves the mission, not individual agendas. Leaders rise by stepping into responsibility, not by stepping over others. And when power is exercised with efficacy, it energizes the system rather than destabilizing it. It signals to employees that advancement is possible for those who perform and contribute, not just for those who play the game. That clarity unleashes trust, motivates high performers to stay, and builds a culture where excellence is not just expected—it's modeled.

- **Strategic traction** – True strategy is the ability to move decisively in the right direction, aligned, adaptive, and accountable. When cultural friction is removed, communication accelerates, execution sharpens, and decision-making becomes more accurate. As a result, the organization gains the agility to respond to change without losing direction, the capacity to innovate ahead of the market, and the discipline to deliver results that position the business ahead of its industry.

- **Cultural congruence** – The values on the wall match the behaviors in the room. People don't waste energy decoding what's real or navigating contradictions. That clarity creates stability, accelerates trust, and strengthens identity—internally and externally. As a result, engagement deepens, brand credibility increases, and the business attracts and retains people and partners who believe in what it stands for.

- **Accountability with trust** – In high-performing cultures, accountability isn't enforced through fear or micromanagement, it's modeled through consistency. Standards are high, but so is trust. Leaders don't avoid hard conversations—they have them early, with purpose and respect. Insights, observations, and information becomes a source of growth, not fear. And because people know where they stand and why it matters, they rise to meet the standard, not out of compliance, but out of pride. Because accountability is practiced with fairness and consistency, teams rise to the occasion. They push one another toward greatness—and still enjoy coming to work.

- **Performance without toxicity** – Results are delivered without burning people out or breaking them down. High-performing cultures don't eliminate pressure—they channel it. Ambition is welcomed. Excellence is welcomed. The environment is demanding, but not depleting. Outcomes are achieved, repeatedly elevating results.

Work feels meaningful because it's effective. The result is a high-functioning system where ambition is respected, performance is sustainable, and toxicity has no foothold. People are energized, not exhausted.

This is what most leaders actually want. They want a business that performs, a culture that lasts, and a team that's both capable and committed.

That doesn't happen because of one great speech or one major transformation effort. It happens through principled and purpose-driven leadership. It happens because leaders tend to the culture as consistently as they pursue the outcomes.

THE PERSONAL REWARDS

There is a kind of freedom that only comes when you stop leading from self-preservation and start leading from purpose.

Transformative leadership isn't just about culture, metrics, or performance. It's about becoming the kind of person who no longer needs to protect, posture, or pretend. It's about walking into difficult rooms without abandoning yourself. It's about knowing, deep down, that who you are and how you lead are no longer in conflict.

This is the reward.

- **You become centered**. Confidence comes from knowing what you're here to do and living it. You move with conviction because your leadership is grounded in a higher mission. Being centered means you're clear on your purpose and intentional about who surrounds you. Your inner circle is made up of individuals bonded by loyalty to becoming the highest version of themselves in what they're building, their contributions, and the difference they are committed to making in the world.

- **You have internal coherence**. Your leadership flows from a place of congruence—where your beliefs, values, and actions are aligned without effort. There is a wholeness to how you show up. You carry a quiet confidence that comes from knowing who you are. Your inner alignment sharpens your judgment, strengthens your presence, and builds the kind of credibility others feel before you speak.

- **You experience deeper resolve**. Every step you take reflects purpose, discipline, and discretion. So when challenges appear or sacrifice is required, there is no dilemma. You move forward without hesitation because each decision has already been made in service of something greater. There is nothing more steadying than knowing you've led with both integrity and efficacy. That defines internal peace. And when you stand in that kind of truth, you don't need to defend it—it proves itself.

- **You shape the future while standing fully in the present**. The impact of your leadership is already unfolding. People are growing because of how you engage them. They are more trustworthy, embrace ownership, and pursue greatness because you've raised the standard. This is the kind of legacy that doesn't wait until the end—it lives in the everyday.

- **You become part of the 10%**. Transformation isn't just what you lead—it's who you are. You've done the work most avoid, made the decisions others hesitate to make, and stayed loyal to your values when it mattered most. That places you among the few who lead with power, purpose, and principle. But the greatest reward isn't just becoming the 10%, it's becoming part of the movement to reverse the statistic. Every choice you make becomes a blueprint for others. Every decision, every conversation, every act of integrity contributes to shifting the standard—until the 10% becomes the norm, not the exception.

This is what it means to be unshaken. Not invincible. Not immune to struggle. But unwilling to abandon the truth—about yourself, your purpose, or the people you serve.

A CULTURAL REVOLUTION

Imagine every individual in your workplace—not just the leaders, but every team member—actively practicing and applying the 5x5. Imagine what becomes possible when vulnerability disarms defensiveness, humility softens arrogance, curiosity replaces impatience, confronting supplants avoidance, and transparency dissolves control.

Now imagine that culture as the lived reality of your organization. The 5x5 is your new culture assessment.

This is not a shift. It's a cultural revolution.

And I say that because I've seen what happens in the absence of it. Across industries and levels, I hear the same two things over and over again, more than any others.

The **#1 question** I receive is: *"Will this be kept confidential?"*

And the **#1 statement** I hear about change is: *"They will never change."*

Remember, the question reveals fear. And the statement reveals resignation. Both are signals that trust is fractured and people have learned to protect themselves—because speaking up often comes with a cost, and hoping for change has led to disappointment.

"Will this be kept confidential?" fades when transparency is modeled from the top, and people experience truth being handled with care—not punishment.

"*They will never change*" dissolves when employees see consistent, principled behavior replacing performative talk, and watch accountability happen in real time.

That's what makes the 5x5 a cultural revolution. Remember, the 5x5 is the origination point: 90% of purpose-driven leaders abandoned their commitment to change because of the left-side behaviors, while the right-side behaviors became the source by which the 10% transformed themselves, their teams, and their organizations.

And you can lead this revolution in your organization. The tools in this book have shown you how. All that is left for you to do is take the first step.

CONCLUSION

THE BEGINNING OF
YOUR JOURNEY

Writing this book came with a great deal of trepidation.

Addressing power and its complexity head-on is risky—it jeopardizes business, to getting hired, and to how you're perceived, especially when you're exposing the patterns that quietly undermine progress while also protecting the people who may still be entangled in them.

There is real risk in naming truths that aren't packaged with soft landings or inspirational slogans—truths that might be perceived as negative simply because they don't flatter or inspire. This tension is familiar to many of us who work closely with leaders, teams, and organizations: can you risk speaking truth without being labeled as negative or stay constructive to neutralize division, without being seen as critical? We've learned the delicacy and the dance to making things substantive without letting them become superficial.

I was extremely intentional about the examples included, and just as intentional about the ones excluded. Many stories were left out deliberately because the individuals involved are still within organizations where sharing their experiences could have consequences.

I was painstakingly careful about what could not be exposed. So, if you've sensed a certain restraint in the storytelling, that's why.

And while these pages may not offer the kind of inspiration that sparkles from the stage, I hope they've offered something better: the kind that quietly stirs something within you as you read. The kind that invites you to step more fully into your power. And confidence you'll recognize when you're standing in the room with your colleagues doing the work, feeling the shift, becoming the leader you were always meant to be.

Based on what I've witnessed firsthand, I've come to see that the most meaningful inspiration doesn't come from words or speeches. Those moments stir briefly, but they fade quickly. The real inspiration rises in the room when one, two, or a few people dive into what's real for them together. It lives in the process, in the vulnerable steps in the middle.

It comes alive when a leader sees themselves clearly for the first time in a long time; when a team finally names what's been unsaid and something broken begins to mend; when false harmony gives way to truth and a breakthrough becomes possible. It's in those raw, honest spaces where the work happens and where the shift begins. That's where true inspiration lives. In those intimate moments, inspiration isn't just felt—it lasts. Long after the room has emptied.

My hope is this book brings you not just insight, but also encouragement—and perhaps even a sense of quiet excitement— to elevate the brightest side of your highest potential by finally making space for the other side of the coin: the parts of ourselves we often keep in the shadows, but that are just as present in leadership and power.

That's when, where, and how the most powerful and positive emotions emerge, not because they were handed to you, but because they were awakened within you.

BEING UNSHAKEN

To stay aligned with your purpose is to face resistance, discomfort, and decisions that others may never understand. But it's also how you build something that lasts. When you lead this way, trust deepens, culture transforms, and your legacy is defined by integrity, not image.

Abandoning that purpose may bring temporary relief. It may help you avoid conflict or protect your standing. But the cost is far greater: lost trust, missed moments, and a legacy that never reached its potential.

Every leader meets a crossroads. Not once, but many times. This book has named that moment for what it truly is: a reckoning between self-preservation and purpose. Between safety and significance. Between protecting what is and stepping into what could be.

And what you choose in that moment isn't just about strategy or outcome—it defines who you are as a leader. That is the weight of it. Because what you tolerate becomes your culture. What you choose becomes your character.

Crossroads don't change but you can. And what they always ask is this: What truth are you willing to face, even if it challenges how you see yourself or those closest to you?

Transformative leaders have already answered that question. They've done the deeper work of leading from within. They are clear on what they stand for and what they will not sacrifice because their leadership is rooted not in ego, but in service to a future worth building.

That kind of clarity stands out. It's unmistakable.

It is unshaken.

And yes—it's unicorn-level rare.

But that rarity is what gives it power. To be the exception is to lead from a place most avoid. And that's exactly why your impact lasts.

When others are reacting from fear or self-interest, the transformative leader stays anchored—in purpose, in principle, and in people.

And when a win comes—especially in uncertain conditions—pause. This is when it's paramount to honor the people and relationships alongside you. Acknowledge those who carried weight, who challenged your thinking, who made you better. In moments of instability, acknowledgment becomes more than gratitude; it becomes congruence. It says, *We did this together. We'll keep going together.*

YOUR NEXT STEPS: EMBODYING TRANSFORMATIVE LEADERSHIP

You've already begun the work. Now it's time to expand it—deepen your practice, sharpen your impact, and lead with even greater clarity and courage.

1. Reconnect with your purpose.

Purpose is your leadership anchor—but it must evolve with you. Ask yourself: Does my purpose still reflect who I am and who I'm becoming? If not, refine it. A true purpose is personal, inspirational, and strong enough to guide you under pressure.

2. Name three principles that protect your purpose.

Purpose inspires, but principles sustain. Identify three non-negotiables that will keep you grounded when your power, position, or identity feels threatened. These must serve the greater good and be actionable—keeping your ego in the back seat and your purpose at the wheel.

3. Practice the 5x5 in real time.

The **5x5 Framework** helps you recognize when you're leading from ego or purpose—*in the moment it matters most.* These five behaviors will keep your leadership uncompromised when fear, pressure, or power distort your instincts. Use them daily, especially when the stakes are high.

4. Move from personal to systemic impact.

You've worked through the Transformation Formula—now it's time for Level 2. The **5 Accelerators** are designed for leaders ready to examine every challenge through a deeper lens. Most challenges trace back to a lack of process and these 5 reflect how the top 10% solved them. Visit DrTiffanyBrandreth.com to go deeper.

5. Recognize the crossroads when they appear.

Every leader encounters moments that make you quietly ask: *Will you serve yourself, or serve something greater?* Don't miss them. The decisions you make at these crossroads will define your leadership more than any role, title, or intention ever will.

REMEMBER THE RIPPLE EFFECT

To be unshaken is to sit inside the tension truth creates and still choose to bring it forward even when you have the power to hide it, because the sacrifice serves the universal, collective good.

Remember, the perceived risk will appear before the reward. I encourage you to have faith. That's the nature of purpose-driven leadership. It requires faith. And it's that faith—demonstrated in the hard moments—that makes your purpose powerful.

You are capable of extraordinary impact. Let your leadership reflect the best of who you are. Every decision you make has the power to leave a legacy that extends far beyond the boundaries of your organization and impact the lives of every person you touch. Trust in the impact of your purpose. Let your principles serve that purpose in every pivotal moment. And let your faith—not fear— guide what comes next.

To be unshaken is not to stand without fear. It's to stand in truth when fear demands you retreat. Because when you choose truth over comfort, you become the steady ground on which others find their courage.

ACKNOWLEDGMENTS

This work would not exist without the extraordinary colleagues whose belief, support, and decisions influenced its course.

To Glenn Sanders, Lauren Cavitt, Annie Toth, and Chris Wilson—Glenn, you were the first person I spoke to about this research, serving as a sounding board when it was only preliminary patterns emerging from the data. You believed in its importance from its inception. Together, the four of you embody what this book is about: courage and principles that upheld a higher purpose over self-preservation and accepting the sacrifice that comes with it. You represent the 10% of transformative leaders. You took a stand when choosing security would have been the incredibly easier, safer, more stable path. That is rare—and you are rare. Your example will stay with me always, admired far beyond what words can express.

To colleagues who became advisors, advocates, and team members on projects over the course of one, two, and even three decades—Jorge Meléndez, Gail Herring, Ishaq Memon (and Glenn, Lauren, and Chris again)—my heartfelt gratitude for your steadfast support, your contributions, and the trust I can place in you without hesitation. To Upavit Savsaviya with GlobPixel—thank you for co-designing all of my leadership models with me, bringing them to life with clarity and distinction, and for the heartwarming partnership we've shared. And to Monique Thompson, your near-daily affirmations, prayers, and quotes are a quiet encouragement throughout this journey, carrying me in ways unseen but deeply felt.

To Robert Gordon—you were the first truly transformative leader I had as a boss. You saw something in me before I saw it in myself. Later, as a mentor you gave me the confidence to coach executives twice my age and helped me see that I was ready to expand my reach in ways I hadn't imagined. It was a catalyst that propelled my career forward from that point on. Thank you for believing in me—it made more of a difference than you'll ever know.

To my parents—thank you for raising me with the values that became the foundation of who I am. I believe my dad has been my greatest teacher of humility, honesty, hard work, and service. I remember when he was selling our big white Suburban for $2,000, parked in the pasture of our front yard so it could be seen by passing drivers. One day, a man stopped and offered him $1,000 in cash—ten crisp $100 bills that he held up in front of him—and said, "You know you can't turn this down." And yet, my dad did. Instead, he sold the car to a family friend for $1. That may not sound like much, but for our family, it was. That example taught me about ego, humanity, and quiet leadership. His integrity shaped who I am—and I carry it with me into every room I enter.

To Aloha Publishing—thank you for your steadfast patience and collaboration. Every time I thought I was done, I wasn't. I think this was the only time when my word absolutely *could not* be counted on. I'm deeply grateful for the grace you extended at every step.

To every instance of resistance I faced while working to create change—you were not a barrier. You've been among the greatest teachers I've ever had. You stretched me, sharpened me, and continue to shape how I lead and learn. The learning and lessons have been immeasurable—and they are the reason this book exists.

To my clients who have become friends, supporters, and advocates—you know who you are. The gift of meeting you, working alongside you, and sharing both laughter and tears has been one of my greatest joys. Your trust has meant more to me than words can capture. You are the reward. The impact we've created together is the reward. It is what makes this journey meaningful, and why I am still here doing this work. Thank you, from the bottom of my heart.

To every individual, executive team, department, and organization I've had the privilege to work with—I am deeply grateful for your trust, your hope, and the opportunities to create meaningful change together. You are co-authors in this work. This book is as much yours as it is mine, and the impact I hope it makes is ours to share.

ABOUT THE AUTHOR

Dr. Tiffany Brandreth is an award-winning recognized expert in power dynamics, leadership transformation, and culture change. An organizational psychologist, consultant, and coach, she brings over two decades of experience in developmental psychology and organizational behavior to her work with senior leaders and executive teams.

Through private, NDA-bound partnerships, she works with C-suite teams and senior executive leaders to align behaviors with values, unlock collective performance, and build healthy cultures that make their vision achievable and sustainable. Her work strengthens leadership at every level by replacing the micro-dynamics that quietly fragment teams with principled habits that accelerate trust, collaboration, and uncompromised decision-making.

She has worked across Global 50 corporations, Fortune 500 companies, private enterprises, family-owned businesses, government agencies, nonprofits, and small enterprises—spanning more than 25 industries. Behind closed doors, she is the trusted advisor leaders call when what's at stake can't be risked publicly, helping them lead the change they believe in.

Dr. Brandreth has trained and coached thousands across the globe. Her 2025 TEDx Talk, ***"How Truth Confronts Purpose-Driven Leaders,"*** explores the pivotal moment when leaders must choose between ego and purpose. Her original research revealed that only 10% of leaders choose purpose when it matters most. Her mission is to help turn that 10% into the 90%. She has been featured in USA Today, NBC, and CEO Today, and is known for turning resistance into results and complexity into confident action.

Her work disrupts conventional leadership development, re-architects how power is held and used, and equips purpose-driven leaders to lead with truth, efficacy, and irreversible transformation.

In addition to her consulting work, Dr. Brandreth is a sought-after keynote speaker and serves as an HR expert witness in employment law cases. She also supports legal teams by developing the human impact narrative in personal injury claims and advising on trial strategy through the lens of juror bias and perception. Whether in the boardroom or the courtroom, she is dedicated to influencing outcomes that cultivate the conditions for real and lasting change.

She lives in Newport Beach, California.

CONNECT WITH ME

★ ★ ★ ★ ★

Love This Book . . . Give a 5-Star Review
If you enjoyed this book, leave a five-star review on Amazon
and help others discover it. Your review is invaluable.

Gift a Book
Gifting a book, ebook, or audiobook could change someone's
life forever. You can gift a book on Amazon very easily.

Empower Your Team and Future Leaders
Purchase copies of this book to inspire your team members, employees, or young entrepreneurs. To order this book in bulk quantities,
email alohapublishing@gmail.com or visit AlohaBookStore.com

Invite Me to Speak
Interested in a speaking engagement at your company,
organization, or conference? Connect with me at
https://www.drtiffanybrandreth.com/contact-1

Discover More
Explore my C-suite services, workshops,
and leadership programs at DrTiffanyBrandreth.com

www.ingramcontent.com/pod-product-compliance
Lightning Source LLC
Chambersburg PA
CBHW072346200326
41519CB00015B/3685